ISBN 978-0-260-60153-7
PIBN 10958847

This book is a reproduction of an important historical work. Forgotten Books uses
state-of-the-art technology to digitally reconstruct the work, preserving the original format
whilst repairing imperfections present in the aged copy. In rare cases, an imperfection in
the original, such as a blemish or missing page, may be replicated in our edition. We do,
however, repair the vast majority of imperfections successfully; any imperfections that
remain are intentionally left to preserve the state of such historical works.

JOURNAL

OF THE

ONE HUNDRED AND NINTH SESSION

OF THE

NORTH CAROLINA ANNUAL CONFERENCE

OF THE

METHODIST PROTESTANT CHURCH

HELD NOVEMBER 4th to NOVEMBER 9th

NINETEEN HUNDRED AND THIRTY-SIX

ALBEMARLE, N. C.

PUBLISHED BY THE SECRETARY

PRICE 25 CENTS

RULES OF ORDER

1. At 2 o'clock on the opening day of Conference, the order shall be reading of the President's Annual Report.

2. At 3 o'clock P. M., on the first day of the session, the officers of the Conference shall be elected by ballot.

3. The President shall take the chair at the hour to which the Conference adjourned and call the Conference to order.

4. Each morning session shall be opened by reading a portion of the Scripture and prayer, under direction of the President.

5. At the meeting of each daily session the Secretary shal read the Minutes of the preceding day, and the Conference correct and prepare them for registration.

6. It shall be the duty of the Chair, or the privilege of a member, to call any brother to order who may indulge in personal reflections or irrelevant debate.

7. The Chair shall decide all questions of order subject to an appeal to the Conference, which appeal shall be decided without debate.

8. All the committees shall be appointed by the Chair, unless otherwise ordered by the Conference.

9. The President may participate in debate by calling a member to the Chair.

10. The President shall vote on no question, except in case of a tie.

11. No member shall speak on any question without rising from his seat and respectfully addressing the Chair as "Mr. President," and being recognized by the Chair.

12. No member shall be allowed to speak more than once on any question, except by unanimous permission of the Conference.

13. No person shall pass between the Chair and a member speaking, or interrupt the speaker, except by permission to explain.

14. Members shall not converse together in a tone sufficiently loud to disturb the Conference.

15. Members shall retain their seats, unless rising to speak, or for the purpose of retiring.

16. Members are required to vote in all cases, unless excused therefrom by the Conference.

17. No motion shall be entertained or debated until the same shall be seconded.

18. All motions and resolutions made and seconded shall be open for debate, except the previous question, the motion to adjourn, and to lay on the table, which questions shall be decided without debate.

19. All amendments shall be disposed of before the vote is taken on the main question.

20. All questions of order arising after the previous question has been called for shall be decided without debate.

21. The decision of all questions shall be Yes or No. The yeas and nays shall be recorded on the journal by the call of one-fifth of the members present.

22. All resolutions or amendments shall be reduced to writing.

23. No motion for reconsideration shall be in order, except made by a member who voted with the majority, and on the same or succeeding day, except by a two-thirds vote of the members present.

24. No motion or resolution indefinitely postponed shall be called up again during the session.

25. No person shall speak more than five minutes without permission of the Conference.

26. No committee shall meet during the session of Conference except by permission.

27. All petitions and resolutions shall be referred to proper committee.

ORDER OF BUSINESS

1. Calling of roll.
2. Devotional service.
3. Reading and correction of minutes
4. Presentation of memorials, petitions.
5. Report of standing committees.
6. Introduction of resolutions.
7. Incidental business.
8. Unfinished business.
9. Incidental business.
10. Unfinished business.

CONFERENCE DIRECTORY

(Figures opposite names indicate number of roll calls answered.
Figures in third column, number of years on roll or in relation.
*Absent.)

Name	Charge	Yrs.	Address
Anderson, J. R. 5	Mt. Hermon	1	Burlington, N. C.
Andrews, R. M. 5	Conf. President	5	High Point, N. C.
Ashburn, W. F. 5	Superannuate	9	Greensboro, N. C.
Auman, J. C. 3	Thomasville, Com.	2	Thomasville, N. C.
Ballard, E. L. 5	Asheville	1	Asheville, N. C.
Bates, C. W.	Haw River	1	Brown Summit, N. C.
Bell, H. W. 5	Rockingham	3	Rockingham, N. C.
Bethea, N. G. 5	West End Gbro	3	Greensboro, N. C.
Bingham, E. A. 4	Saxapahaw	2	Saxapahaw, N. C.
Bingham, P. E. *	Without appmnt	2	Savannah, Ga.
Bowman, J. T. 5	Denton	4	Denton, N. C.
Braxton, J. W. 5	Mt. Pleasant	4	Liberty, N. C.
Broome, D. D. *	Without appmnt	3	Charlotte, N. C.
Brown, Geo. R. 5	Reidsville	11	Reidsville, N. C.
Burgess, J. A. 5	Flat Rock	1	Stokesdale, N. C.
Carroll, J. E. 5	Grace, Greensboro	4	Greensboro, N. C.
Casto, Homer *	Supt. Bethel Home	18	Weaverville, N. C.
Cook, Earl A. 4	Roberta	4	Concord, N. C.
Cowan, E. G. 5	Seagrove-Love Joy	3	Seagrove, N. C.
Cranford, J. D. 4	Vance	3	Henderson, N. C.
Curry, G. L. 5	Spring Church	2	Pleasant Hill, N. C.
Dixon, A. G. 5	Supt. Children's Ho	9	High Point, N. C.
Ferree, G. B. 5	West Forsyth	3	Tobaccoville, N. C.
Fogleman, H. F. 3	Orange	1	Efland, N. C.
Forlines, C. E. 2	Pres., W. T. Sem	2	Westminster, Md.
Garlington, J. E.	Midway	2	High Point, N. C.
Garner, D. I. 5	Mebane	1	Mebane, N. C.
Gibbs, F. L. 1	Sec. Brd. Rel. Edu	10	Pittsburgh, Pa.
Grant, C. L. 4	Davidson	2	Denton, N. C.
Harkey, W. L. 5	Lincolnton	1	Lincolnton, N. C.
Harrison, N. M. 2	Prom. Sec. H. P. Col.	7	High Point, N. C.
Helms, L. S. 3	Shelby-Caroleen	1	Shelby, N. C.
Henderson, M. C. 4	Richland	3	Asheboro, N. C.
Hendry, G. H. 3	Charlotte, First	5	Charlotte, N. C.
Hethcox, R. L. 5	Mocksville	3	Mocksville, N. C.
Hill, C. H. 4	Why Not	3	High Point, N. C.
Holmes, G. W. 5	Superannuate	10	Graham, N. C.
Howard, W. M. 5	Halifax	2	Enfield, N. C.
Hunter, A. L. *	Superannuate	3	Pinnacle, N. C.
Hunter, R. A. 4	Forsyth	6	Winston-Salem, N. C.
Huss, D. T. 4	Kannapolis	1	Kannapolis, N. C.

CONFERENCE DIRECTORY—Continued

Name	Charge	Yrs.	Address
Hutton, J. R. 5	Lebanon, H. Pt	2	High Point, N. C.
Isley, C. G. 5	Albemarle, First	2	Albemarle, N. C.
Isley, H. L. 4	Alamance	3	Burlington, N. C.
Johnson, T. M. 5	Anderson	1	Easley, S. C.
Joyner, Q. L. 3	In hands President	1	Newton, N. C.
Kennett, P. S. 1	Prof. H. P. Col	13	High Point, N. C.
Lamb, E. A. 5	Tabernacle-Julian	2	Greensboro, N. C.
Lindley, A. O. 5	Chatham	1	Liberty, N. C.
Lindley, P. E	Prof. H. P. Col	13	High Point, N. C.
Love, F. R. 5	Pleasant Grove	2	Thomasville, N. C.
Love, J. L. 4	Draper	1	Draper, N. C.
Loy, D. M. *	Superannuate	6	Glen Raven, N. C.
Loy, O. C. 2	Thomasville, First	2	Thomasville, N. C.
Loy, W. M. 1	Without Appmnt	1	Burlington, N. C.
Mabry, L. E. 5	Lexington, First	2	Lexington, N. C.
Madison, J. C. 4	High Point, First	4	High Point, N. C.
Madison, T. G. 4	Cleveland	2	Lawndale, N. C.
McCulloch, T. F. 3	Superannuate	17	Greensboro, N. C.
McDowell, W. F. 4	Super., Richland	15	Asheboro, N. C.
Millaway, G. F. *	Superannuate	6	Greensboro, N. C.
Minnis, J. F. 2	Missionary, India	1	Dhulia, W. K., India
Morgan, J. M. 5	Greensville	2	Triplet, Va.
Morris, J. D. 3	Pinnacle-Mt. Zion	3	Pinnacle, N. C.
Neese, W. H. 5	N. Davidson	2	Winston-Salem, N. C.
Paschall, F. W. 5	Burlington, First	7	Burlington, N. C.
Peeler, E. O. 5	Concord	1	Concord, N. C.
Pegg, J. P. 4	Lexington, State St.	2	Lexington, N. C.
Pike, W. M. 4	Superannuate	10	Liberty, N. C.
Powell, H. L. 3	Superannuate	2	Thomasville, N. C.
Pritchard, J. E. 5	Calvary, Greensboro	4	Greensboro, N. C.
Reed, W. D. 3	Superannuate	1	Greensboro, N. C.
Reynolds, G. L. *	Randolph	3	High Point, N. C.
Ridge, Atlas 2	In hands President	3	Lexington, N. C.
Ridge, C. E. 5	Shiloh	4	Lexington, N. C.
Shelton, A. D. 2	Greensboro, St. Paul	3	Greensboro, N. C.
Short, J. R. 3	Mecklenburg	2	Matthews, N. C.
Spencer, C. L. 5	Granville	8	Henderson, N. C.
Stubbins, R. C. 5	Gibsonville	3	Gibsonville, N. C.
Suits, Edward 5	High Pt. Rankin Ml.	3	High Point, N. C.
Surratt, H. F. 5	Graham	2	Graham, N. C.
Taylor, S. W. 4	Asheboro	3	Asheboro, N. C.
Thompson, H. S. B. *	Superannuate	9	Roanoke Rapids, N. C.
Totten, W. T. *	Superannuate	5	Yadkin College, N. C.
Trogdon, J. B. 4	Randleman	6	Randleman, N. C.

Trolinger, J. H. 5........Littleton ....1 Littleton, N. C.
Trollinger, J. L. 5........Winston-Salem, First.1 Winston-Salem, N. C.
Troxler, R. S. 2............Haw Riv-Glen Raven.2 Burlington, N. C.
Vickery, R. L. 5............Fr'ndship-Love's Gr...1 Albemarle, N. C.
Way, C. B. 5..............Guilford ....1 Jamestown, N. C.
Whitehead, T. J. 4........Henderson ....1 Henderson, N. C.
Williams, B. M. 5........Fallston ....1 Fallston, N. C.
Williams, D. R. 3........Enfield-Whitakers .....1 Enfield, N. C.
Williams, J. D. 5..........High Pt. Welch Ml.....6 High Point, N. C.
Williams, J. S. *..........Chap. Mis. G. Sam...26 Asheville, N. C.
Williams, O. B. 5..........Kernersville-S. Win....3 Kernersville, N. C.
Williams, T. A. *.........Superannuate ....1 High Point, N. C.

ACTIVE PREACHERS

Clark, W. C. 5..............Dem-Weaverville.........2 Asheville, N. C.
Easter, O. L. 5.............Creswell ....2 Creswell, N. C.
Hamilton, E. P. 5.........Mt. Zion ....2 High Point, N. C.
Holt, K. G. 5................Yarborough ....3 Cross Anchor, S. C.
Moser, R. E. L. 5........Burlington, Ft. Pl......1 Burlington, N. C.
Morris, C. P. 3.............Danville ....3 Danville, Va.
Pittard, Leo 3..............Moriah-B. Summit......2 Brown Summit, N. C.
Smith, Aubert 5...........Liberty-Siler City.......2 Liberty, N. C.
Yokeley, Herman ....Connelly Springs ....2 High Point, N. C.
Wright, F. A................Spencer-China Grove..1 High Point, N. C.

HONORARY MEMBERS

Humphreys, G. I..........President, H. P. Col..7 High Point, N. C.
Spahr, S. K.................Pas. Emeritus, Gr....10 Greensboro, N. C.

OFFICERS OF THE ANNUAL CONFERENCE

President
REV. R. M. ANDREWS, D.D., High Point, N. C.

Secretary
REV. C. W. BATES; D.D., Brown Summit, N. C.

Assistant Secretary
REV. F. W. PASCHALL, S.T.D., Burlington, N. C.

Treasurer
MR. J. H. ALLEN, Reidsville, N. C.

Statistical Secretary
REV. E. G. COWAN, Seagrove, N. C.

Press Representative
REV. J. L. TROLLINGER, Winston-Salem, N. C.

Conference Historian
REV. J. ELWOOD CARROLL, Greensboro, N. C.

Keeper of Records
REV. PAUL S. KENNETT, LL.D., High Point, N. C.

OFFICERS OF THE GENERAL CONFERENCE

President
REV. JAS. H. STRAUGHN, D.D., Baltimore, Md.

Secretary
REV. C. W. BATES, D.D., Brown Summit, N. C.

Assistant Secretary
REV. J. S. EDDINS, Birmingham, Ala.

Treasurer
MR. H. C. STALEY, Baltimore, Md.

CONFERENCE BOARDS AND COMMITTEES

Conference Trustees
1937—J. R. Hutton, G. L. Reynolds.
1938—Geo. R. Brown, L. L. Wren.
1939—M. A. Coble, Edward Suits.
1940—W. F. Ashburn, J. Norman Wills.

Boundary Committee
1937—G. L. Curry, L. L. Wren, C. L. Berrier.
1938—N. G. Bethea.
1939—S. W. Taylor.
1940—R. M. Andrews, Edward Suits.

Board of Church Extension
1937—W. L. Ward, L. M. Foust.
1938—J. E. Pritchard, S. W. Taylor, G. L. Curry.
1939—W. A. Davies, W. F. Redding, Jr.

Annual Conference Council of Religious Education
1937—J. W. Braxton.
1938—P. E. Lindley.

Commission on Methodist Cooperation
1937—L. F. Ross, S. W. Taylor.
1938—C. W. Bates.
1939—W. T. Hanner, R. M. Andrews.

Trustees of High Point College
President of the North Carolina Annual Conference, Methodist Protestant Church—R. M. Andrews, D. D.

President of High Point College—G. I. Humphreys, D. D.

1936—J. D. Williams, D. D., J. M. Millikan, J. N. Wills, Dr. J. T. Burrus, F. Logan Porter.

1937—Rev. J. C. Auman, C. F. Finch, W. L. Ward, H. A. Millis, C. H. Kearns.

1938—Rev. N. M. Harrison, C. C. Robbins, J. S. Pickett, R. T. Amos, O. A. Kirkman.

1939—S. W. Taylor, D. D, L. F. Ross, Mrs. M. J. Wrenn, R. O. Lindsay, A. M. Rankin.

1940—J. E. Pritchard, D.D., R. M. Cox, Dr. J. H. Cutchin, W. F. Hunsucker.

College Committee of Ten—Mrs. D. S. Coltrane, Mrs. M. A. Coble, Mrs. J. H. Cutchin, L. F. Ross, A. J. Koonce, J. T. Warlick, Revs. J. E. Pritchard, C. E. Ridge, H. F. Surratt, B. M. Williams.

Directors of Pastors' Summer School
1937—T. M. Johnson;
1938—J. E. Carroll, T. G. Madison;
1940—S. W. Taylor.

North Carolina Board of Education—Rev. T. M. Johnson, D.D., President; Rev. J. E. Pritchard, D.D., Vice-President; Dr. C. R. Hinshaw, Secretary-Treasurer; Mr. J. H. Allen, Rev. R. M. Andrews, D.D., Rev. C. W. Bates, D.D., Mr. R. C. Causey, Mr. J. M. Cutchin, Jr., Mr. W. T. Hanner, Mr. J. B. Hicks, Mr. V. W. Idol, Dr. F. W. Paschall, Mr. J. S. Pickett, Rev. S. W. Taylor, D.D., Mr. J. Norman Wills, Mr. L. L. Wren, Mr. J. G. Rogers, Dr. G. I. Humphreys, (Honorary).

Trustees of the Children's Home—J. M. Millikan, Chairman, Greensboro, N. C.; A. M. Rankin, Secretary-Treasurer, High Point, N. C.; Mrs. A. G. Dixon, High Point, N. C.; Geo. T. Penny, High Point, N. C.; J. C. Penny, Charlotte, N. C.; G. J. Cherry, Charleston, S. C.; Mrs. W. C. Hammer, Asheboro, N. C.; C. F. Finch, Thomasville, N. C.; Mrs. R. M. Cox, Winston-Salem, N. C.; Mrs. H. C. Nicholson, Mebane, N. C.; Mr. J. G. Rogers, Burlington, N. C.; Mr. J. D. Ross, Asheboro, N. C.; Mr. Lonnie McPherson, Graham, N. C.; J. W. Montgomery, High Point, N. C.; Rev. J. C. Broomfield, D.D., Fairmont, W. Va.; the President of the North Carolina Annual Conference, Ex-Officio, the pastor of First Church, High Point, Honorary.

Superintendent of the Children's Home—A. G. Dixon.

Board of Managers Superannuated Fund Society—T. M. Johnson, J. A. Burgess, S. R. Harris, J. D. Williams, Edward Suits, J. Norman Wills, L. L. Wren, T. J. Whitehead.

Trustees of the District Parsonage—J. Norman Wills, J. M. Millikan, F. R. Stout, W. T. Hanner.

Committee on Religious Education—J. C. Auman, J. E. Carroll, Geo. R. Brown, N. G. Bethea, R. C. Stubbins.

Committee on Evangelism—F. W. Paschall, L. E. Mabry, A. D. Shelton, G. H. Hendry, E. A. Cook.

Committee Advisory to the President—A. G. Dixon, J. D. Williams, J. C. Madison, R. C. Stubbins, F. W. Paschall.

Committee on Rural Church—J. W. Braxton, J. T. Bowman, G. L. Curry, C. B. Baskett, Wilberforce Causey.

Committee on Financial Recommendations—R. M. Andrews, G. I. Humphreys, J. E. Pritchard, A. G. Dixon, T. M. Johnson, T. J. Whitehead, W. L. Ward.

Committee on Stewardship—N. G. Bethea, Geo. R. Brown, J. G. Rogers.

Committee on Nominations—E. O. Peeler, E. A. Bingham, C. G. Isley.

OTHER APPOINTMENTS

United Dry Forces—Edward Suits, Dr. J. A. Pickett.

North Carolina Council of Churches—P. E. Lindley, N. G. Bethea, F. W. Paschall.

Southern Inter-racial Commission—J. G. Madison, J. E. Carroll.

Fraternal Messengers—Blue Ridge-Atlantic, M. E. Church—J. E. Carroll. North Carolina, M. E., South—T. J. Whitehead. Western North Carolina, M. E., South—C. W. Bates.

To Preach Conference Sermon—C. E. Ridge.

To Preach Ordination Sermon—P. S. Kennett.

To Audit Books of Conference Treasurer—E. L. Somers, C. J. Roberts.

and Mrs. H. W. Mitchell.

Church Music—Ministers: J. W. Braxton, W. M. Howard, F. R. Love, R. A. Hunter, A. O. Lindley; Lay members: Miss Lucy Rogers, Mrs. J. H. Cutchin, T. Worth Trogdon, J. H. Speas, D. R. Connell, and Miss Lelia Byerly.

Methodist Protestant Herald—Ministers: T. G. Madison, C. E. Ridge, D. R. Williams, O. C. Loy, C. B. Way; Lay members: L. L. Wren, Dr. W. C. Goley, Mrs. J. B. Gregson, W. A. Davies, and A. N. Linville.

Fraternal Relations—Ministers: E. O. Peeler, O. L. Easter, J. D. Cranford, K. G. Holt, J. L. Love; Lay members: E. E. Wagner, M. E. Marlow, M. J. Setzer, C. A. Harkey, and J. P. Baldwin.

Missions—Ministers: J. C. Auman, J. P. Pegg, J. R. Anderson, G. L. Reynolds, J. R. Hutton; Lay members: Adrian Perry, Mrs. C. H. Davenport, Mrs. W. W. Eldridge, T. S. Coble, E. P. Dwiggins, and Mrs. J. M. Baity.

Official Character—Ministers: T M. Johnson, J. D. Williams, G. R. Brown, R. C. Stubbins, Edward Suits; Lay members: D. M. Davidson, L. H. Sides, R. A. Lackey, J. F. Williams, and E. H. Reynolds.

Parsonages—Ministers: E. A. Bingham. C. L. Grant, B. M. Williams, C. L. Spencer, T. A. Williams; Lay members: Mrs. E. C. Walters, Miss Daisy Porter, Miss Ruby Thompson, B. F. Baxter, and J. M. Deviney.

President's Message—Ministers: J. A. Burgess, F. W. Paschall, N. G. Bethea, J. C. Madison, J. M. Morgan; Lay members: Dr. John Swaim, F. R. Stout, C. C. Robbins, O. G. Carpenter, and F. D. Hamilton.

Social Service—Ministers: H. F. Surratt, J. T. Bowman, J. R. Short, L. S. Helms; Lay members: Mrs. J. S. Moore, L. W. Causey, W. L. Holt, C. H. Smith, and C. L. Berrier.

Pastoral Work—Ministers: S. W. Taylor, W. H. Neese, J. H. Trolinger, R. L. Vickery, W. L. Harkey, and G. B. Ferree; Lay members: J. M. Teague, J. S. Wade, J. W. Johnson, F. F. Briggs, A. C. Harris and C. F. Jobe.

Ordinances—Ministers: J. D. Morris, H. W. Bell, Leo Pittard, R. L. Moser, D. T. Huss; Lay members: W. T. Howell, Russell Clinard, P. M. Gordon, W. T. Coble, L. B. Silvers, and H. W. Sneed.

Obituary Committee for Rev. W. F. Kennett—Revs. J. E. Pritchard, W. F. Ashburn and Mr. J. Norman Wills.

Pulpit Supply—C. G. Isley, D. I. Garner, W. D. Reed, E. A. Cook, and J. H. Harkey.

CONFERENCE FACULTY

S. W. TAYLOR, *Chairman*

H. F. SURRATT, *Secretary*

First Year

J. D. WILLIAMS (1940)—"Personal Salvation." (Tillet)
S. W. TAYLOR (1937)—"Introduction to the Study of the Bible." (Van Pelt)
R. C. STUBBINS (1938)—"The Ministers Week-day Challenge." (Byington)
T. M. JOHNSON (1936) "Objectives in Religious Education." (Vieth)
H. F. SURRATT (1937)—"Principles of Preaching." (Davis)
GEO. R. BROWN (1939)—"The Discipline."
J. A. BURGESS (1939)—"Robert's Rules of Order."
G. W. HOLMES (1940)—Presentation of one fully written original Sermon on Repentence. Required parallel: Davis Democratic Methodism.

Second Year

B. M. WILLIAMS (1939)—Old Testament History. (Wade)
R. M. ANDREWS (1937)—"The Christian Faith." First half. (Curtis)
A. G. DIXON (1940)—"The Christian Preacher." (Garvie)
G. L. REYNOLDS (1938)—"The Curriculum of Religious Education." (Betts)
C. W. BATES (1939)—"History of the Christian Church." First half. (Qualben)
F. W. PASCHAL (1938)—"The Christian Message and Program." (McAfee)
J. E. PRITCHARD (1937)—The Discipline and Robert's Rules of Order.
T. M. JOHNSON (1939)—Presentation of one fully written sermon on Regeneration. Required parallel; "Divine Credentials." (Lewis)

Third Year

J. R. HUTTON (1940)—"New Testament History." (Rall)
H. L. ISLEY (1938)—"The Christian Faith." Second half. (Curtis)
J. E. CARROLL (1938)—"Teaching Religion." (Myers)
G. L. CURRY (1937)—"Church Administration." (Leach)
R. A. HUNTER (1940)—"Life of Christ." (Smith)
GEO. R. BROWN (1939)—Presentation of one fully written original sermon on Evangelism. Required Parallel, "Human Nature and the Church." (Lindley)

Committee on Entrance: T. M. Johnson, H. F. Surratt, President of the Conference and Chairman of the Faculty.

ROLL OF THE HONORED DEAD

Reg. No.	NAME	Ordained	Died
1	William Bellamy	....	1846
2	James Hunter	....	1831
3	Albritton Jones	....	1845
4	William Price	....	1832
5	Asa Steeley	....	....
6	Thomas Steeley	....	....
7	Alexander Albright	....	1843
8	Henry Bradford	....	1843
9	Jesse H. Cobb	....	....
10	Isaac Coe	....	....
11	John Coe	....	1852
12	Richardson Davidson	....	1845
13	Caswell Drake	....	1861
14	Alson Gray, D. D.	....	1880
15	Joshua Swift	....	....
16	Swain Swift	....	1831
17	William Blair	....	....
18	John Moore	....	1840
19	Christine Allen	....	....
20	Thomas Y. Cook	....	....
21	James Hunt	....	1848
22	Travis Jones	....	....
23	Samuel J. Harris	....	1839
24	Alexander Robbins	....	1868
25	John F. Speight	....	1860
26	Wm. H. Wills, D. D.	1835	1889
27	Joseph Holmes	....	....
28	H. A. Burton	....	....
29	Thomas L. Carter	....	....
30	James Deans	....	....
31	Arrington Gray	....	1846
32	John Lambeth	....	1846
33	Ira E. Norman	....	1857
34	Robert R. Prather	....	1881
35	C. F. Harris, D. D.	1846	1896
36	John Hinshaw	....	1868
37	John Paris, D. D.	....	1883
38	B. L. Hoskins	....	1860
39	A. C. Harris, M. D.	1847	1889
40	J. L. Michaux, D. D.	....	1898
41	G. A. T. Whitaker	1842	1885
42	W. J. Ogburn	....	1860
43	A. W. Lineberry, D. D.	....	1899

ROLL OF THE HONORED DEAD

Reg. No.	NAME	Ordained	Died
44	Andrew Pickens	....	1860
45	Joseph Causey	....	1878
46	J. W. Heath	....	1913
47	R. R. Michaux	....	1899
48	John Gordon	....	1862
49	John C. Forbis	....	1862
50	R. W. Pegram	....	1885
51	R. H. Wills	....	1891
52	J. C. Dean	....	1890
53	J. R. Ball	....	1893
54	S. P. J. Harris	....	1889
55	W. C. Kennett	....	1925
56	W. McB. Roberts	....	1867
57	N. R. Fail	....	1866
58	H. W. Peebles	1862	1892
59	C. A. Pickens	....	1908
60	J. S. Dunn	1868	1908
61	John L. Swain	....	1880
62	A. J. Laughlin	....	1886
63	G. E. Hunt	....	1926
65	W. C. Hammer	1868	1909
66	Henry Lewallen	....	....
67	Jordan Rominger	....	1872
68	D. A. Highfill	1874	1927
69	T. T. Ferree, M. D.	1875	1904
70	John G. Whitfield, D. D.	....	1879
71	W. W. Amick	1874	1907
72	R. R. Hanner	....	1899
73	S. Simpson, D. D.	1879	1912
74	P. D. Moore	....	....
75	G. W. Bowman	....	1908
76	D. A. Fishel	1879	1933
77	W. P. Martin		1929
78	J. H. Totten	....	1905
79	J. M. Wood	....	1881
80	I. I. York	....	1925
81	J. E. Hartsell	....	1912
82	John N. Garrett	1882	1912
83	W. L. Harris	1888	1910
84	W. F. Kennett	1887	1936
86	J. H. Moton	1887	1929
88	J. W. Simpson	....	1893
89	W. E. Swain, D. D.	1884	1923

94	W. A. Bunch	1888	1907
95	C. A. Cecil	1889	1921
96	S. A. Cecil	....	1896
97	C. L. Whitaker, D. D.	1888	1926
100	W. R. Lowdermilk	1900	1917
101	J. H. Stowe	1893	1927
104	C. E. M. Raper	1895	1915
105	W. C. Lassiter	1893	1923
106	W. F. Ohrum	....	1892
107	C. C. Stuart	....	1892
108	Wm. D. Fogleman	1897	1914
109	J. L. Giles	1867	1911
111	C. H. Whitaker	1896	1935
112	D. A. Braswell	1893	1927
115	J. R. Walton	....	1897
118	J. F. McCulloch, D. D.	1893	1934
122	E. G. Lowdermilk	1898	1935
123	J. H. Bowman	1899	1926
126	J. H. Gilbreath	....	....
131	J. T. Turner	....	1911
133	C. J. Edwards	1907	1933
145	L. H. Hatley	1912	1915
148	L. W. Gerringer, D. D.	1913	1934
158	J. B. O'Briant	1917	1930
167	J. W. Hulin	1919	1934
186	J. W. Quick	1924	1926
189	N. Brittain	1925	1930
195	M. P. Chambliss	1926	1934
200	R. E. Andrews	1914	1932
226	C. W. Saunders	1931	1934

CONFERENCE ROLL

Reg. No.	NAME	Admitted	Ordained
74	T. F. McCulloch	1876	1878
85	W. F. McDowell	1883	1888
87	W. M. Pike	1883	1887
93	W. T. Totten	1885	1888
98	A. L. Hunter	1889	1896
102	W. F. Ashburn	1890	1893
103	G. F. Millaway	1890	1893
110	J. R. Hutton	1892	1895
113	T. M. Johnson	1893	1893
114	H. S. B. Thompson	1893	1895
115	J. D. Williams	1893	1896
117	J. S. Williams	1893	1893
120	R. M. Andrews	1896	1898
121	N. G. Bethea	1896	1902
124	C. E. Forlines	1897	1897
125	H. L. Powell	1898	1899
127	A. G. Dixon	1901	1901
128	G. W. Holmes	1901	1903
129	G. L. Reynolds	1901	1910
130	Edward Suits	1901	1907
132	J. A. Burgess	1902	1907
136	W. D. Reed	1904	1907
138	A. O. Lindley	1906	1907
139	Geo. L. Curry	1907	1907
140	S. W. Taylor	1907	1907
141	R. C. Stubbins	1908	1911
143	C. W. Bates	1908	1913
144	T. A. Williams	1908	1912
146	Robert S. Troxler	1910	1912
147	J. E. Pritchard	1912	1912
151	D. R. Williams	1909	1915
153	D. M. Loy	1907	1916
154	Geo. R. Brown	1917	*
155	O. B. Williams	1913	1916
156	Paul S. Kennett	1917	1917
159	A. D. Shelton	1912	1917
160	B. M. Williams	1916	1917
161	H. F. Fogleman	1917	1918
162	R. A. Hunter	1917	1918
163	W. H. Neese	1913	1918
164	H. F. Surratt	1917	1918
165	C. L. Spencer	1919	*
166	N. M. Harrison	1919	1919
168	J. M. Morgan	1915	1919

CONFERENCE ROLL

Reg. No.	NAME	Admitted	Ordained
169	J. B. Trogdon	1911	1919
170	J. C. Auman	1920	1921
171	Homer Casto	1920	1921
173	J. F. Minnis	1922	1922
174	E. A. Bingham	1922	1922
177	H. L. Isley	1923	1923
180	G. H. Hendry	1924	*
181	E. L. Ballard	1924	*
182	P. E. Lindley	1917	1924
183	J. D. Morris	1913	1924
184	F. W. Paschall	1922	1924
187	Atlas Ridge	1921	1924
191	J. R. Anderson	1926	*
194	E. G. Cowan	1921	1925
196	D. I. Garner	1919	1926
197	J. R. Short	1920	1926
198	J. L. Trollinger	1921	1926
202	F. L. Gibbs	1925	1927
203	C. H. Hill	1922	1927
204	C. E. Ridge	1924	1927
207	M. C. Henderson	1926	1928
208	O. C. Loy	1924	1928
209	W. M. Loy	1923	1928
210	J. H. Trolinger	1917	1928
211	C. B. Way	1925	1928
213	J. W. Braxton	1925	1929
214	J. E. Carroll	1925	1929
215	J. D. Cranford	1925	1929
216	L. S. Helms	....	1929
217	P. E. Bingham	1925	1930
218	C. G. Isley	1925	1930
219	F. R. Love	1925	1930
220	T. G. Madison	1925	1930
221	T. J. Whitehead	1928	1930
222	D. D. Broome	....	1931
223	G. B. Ferree	1927	1931
224	Q. L. Joyner	1927	1931
225	J. P. Pegg	1927	1931
227	H. W. Bell	1927	1932
228	C. L. Grant	1927	1932
229	J. L. Love	1927	1932
230	E. O. Peeler	1926	1932
231	R. L. Vickery	1928	1932

CONFERENCE ROLL

Reg. No.	NAME	Admitted	Ordained
232	J. T. Bowman	1933	1933
233	Earl A. Cook	1928	1933
234	R. L. Hethcox	1915	1933
235	D. T. Huss	1933	1933
236	L. E. Mabry	1930	1934
237	J. C. Madison	1930	1934
238	E. A. Lamb	1933	1935
239	W. M. Howard, Jr.	1930	1936
240	J. E. Garlington	1936	*

* By Transfer.

CONFERENCE WIDOWS' DIRECTORY

Name	Address	Husband
Andrews, Mrs. Nora	High Point, N. C.	Rev. R. E. Andrews
Brittain, Mrs. Bessie	Hickory, N. C.	Rev. N. Brittain
Braswell, Mrs.	Pageland, S. C.	Rev. D. A. Braswell
Cecil, Mrs.	High Point, N. C.	Rev. C. A. Cecil
Dosier, Mrs. Mary	Greensboro, N. C.	Rev. J. F. Dosier
Edwards, Mrs. Alice	Washington, N. C.	Rev. C. J. Edwards
Ferree, Mrs.	High Point, N. C.	Rev. T. T. Ferree
Gerringer, Mrs. Mary	Greensboro, N. C.	Rev. L. W. Gerringer
Hulin, Mrs. Sarah	Queen, N. C.	Rev. J. W. Hulin
Hunt, Mrs. Sarah	Lexington, N. C.	Rev. G. E. Hunt
Kennett, Mrs. Ella	Greensboro, N. C.	Rev. W. F. Kennett
Kennett, Mrs. Mary	Greensboro, N. C.	Rev. W. C. Kennett
Lassiter, Mrs.	Rocky Mount, Va.	Rev. W. C. Lassiter
Lowdermilk, Mrs.	Greenville, S. C.	Rev. W. R. Lowdermilk
Lowdermilk, Mrs. Nannie	Liberty, N. C.	Rev. E. G. Lowdermilk
Martin, Mrs.	Lenior, N. C.	Rev. W. P. Martin
O'Briant, Mrs.	Rosemary, N. C.	Rev. J. B. O'Briant
Quick, Mrs.	Pageland, S. C.	Rev. J. W. Quick
Saunders, Mrs. Myrtle	Abner, N. C.	Rev. C. W. Saunders
Whitaker, Mrs.	High Point, N. C.	Rev. C. L. Whitaker
Whitaker, Mrs. Elizabeth	Winston-Salem, N. C.	Rev. C. H. Whitaker

ROLL OF DELEGATES—109th SESSION, ALBEMARLE, N. C.

(Figure opposite names—roll calls answered. *Absent.)

Charge	Name	Address
Alamance	Lillie Mae Braxton 4	Graham, N. C.
Albemarle	J. H. Harkey 5	Albemarle, N. C.
Anderson	H. R. McClimon 3	Greer, S. C.
Asheboro	Dr. John Swaim 2	Asheboro, N. C.
Asheville	L. S. Neville 4	Asheville, N. C.
Bess Chapel	B. F. Baxter *	Cherryville, N. C.
Bessemer City	J. P. Baldwin *	Bessemer City, N. C.
Brown Summit	R. A. Shelton *	Brown Summit, N. C.
Burlington, First	H. B. Cole 4	Burlington, N. C.
Burlington, Ft. Pl.	C. B. Amick 2	Burlington, N. C.
Caroleen-Shelby	Goldie Upton *	Avondale, N. C.
Charlotte, First	Mrs. C. S. Womack 3	Charlotte, N. C.
Chase City		
Chatham	W. M. Pike, Jr. *	Liberty, N. C.
Cleveland	J. M. Diviney 1	Casar, N. C.
Concord	L. H. Sides 3	Concord, N. C.
Connelly Springs	Mrs. J. C. Watson 5	Connelly Springs, N. C.
Creswell	A. W. Davenport 4	Creswell, N. C.
Danville	Hugh Yeatts 4	Danville, N. C.
Davidson	A. C. Harris 3	Eldorado, N. C.
Democrat	David Carter *	Democrat, N. C.
Denton	P. D. Hamilton 5	Denton, N. C.
Draper	W. T. Howell 4	Draper, N. C.
Enfield	S. C. Whitaker 5	Enfield, N. C.
Fallston	R. A. Lackey 3	Fallston, N. C.
Flat Rock	E. P. Dwiggins 5	Kernersville, N. C.
Friendship	C. A. Harkey 4	Albemarle, N. C.
Forsythe	Russell Clinard 4	Winston-Salem, N. C.
Gibsonville	D. M. Davidson *	Gibsonville, N. C.
Glen Raven	T. S. Coble *	Haw River, N. C.
Graham	J. L. Amick 3	Graham, N. C.
Granville	Miss Lucy Rogers 4	Oxford, N. C.
Greensboro, Calvary	J. F. Williams 4	Greensboro, N. C.
Grace	D. S. Coltrane 2	Greensboro, N. C.
St. Paul	J. S. Wade 1	Greensboro, N. C.
West End	Mrs. W. W. Eldridge 4	Greensboro, N. C.
Greensville	J. B. Clements 4	Pairs Store, Va.
Guilford	J. W. Johnson 3	High Point, N. C.
Halifax	Mrs. H. W. Mitchell 5	Littleton, N. C.
Haw River	P. M. Gordon 2	Brown Summit, N. C.
Henderson	Mrs. J. M. Baity 4	Henderson, N. C.
High Point, First	C. C. Robbins 1	High Point, N. C.
Lebanon	F. F. Briggs 5	High Point, N. C.
Rankin Ml	M. J. Setzer 1	High Point, N. C.
Welch Ml	J. T. Morgan 4	High Point, N. C.
Kannapolis	M. E. Marlow 4	Kannapolis, N. C.
Kernersville-S. Win	A. N. Linville *	Kernersville, N. C.
Lexington, First	A. E. Cutting 4	Lexington, N. C.
State Street	E. E. Wagner 4	Lexington, N. C.
Liberty	Mrs. J. B. Gregson 4	Liberty, N. C.
Lincolnton	O. G. Carpenter 2	Lincolnton, N. C.
Littleton	Miss Daisy Porter 5	Littleton, N. C.
Mebane	C. F. Jobe *	Mebane, N. C.

ROLL OF DELEGATES

(Continued)

Charge	Name	Address
Mecklenburg	Chas. Flowe 3	Mathews, N. C.
Midland	J. E. Jenkins 4	Stanfield, N. C.
Midway	Mrs. E. C. Walters 5	Greensboro, N. C.
Mocksville	Lelia Martin 4	Mocksville, N. C.
Moriah	J. F. Jobe 5	Greensboro, N. C.
Mt. Hermon	W. T. Coble 5	Graham, N. C.
Mt. Pleasant	L. W. Causey 4	Liberty, N. C.
Mt. Zion	John Patton 2	Trinity, N. C.
North Davidson	H. P. Berrier 1	Winston-Salem, N. C.
Orange	W. A. Davies 3	Hillsboro, N. C.
Pensacola	L. B. Silvers *	Pensacola, N. C.
Pinnacle-Mt. Zion	F. G. Fowler 2	Pinnacle, N. C.
Pleasant Grove	Clyde Payne 5	Thomasville, N. C.
Porter	Ruby Thompson 5	Albemarle, N. C.
Randleman	J. H. Skeen 5	Randleman, N. C.
Randolph	G. R. Hemphill 3	Julian, N. C.
Reidsville	J. H. Allen 5	Reidsville, N. C.
Richland	Raymond Allred 2	Cedar Falls, N. C.
Roberta	J. Ivey Cline	Concord, N. C.
Rockingham	H. W. Snead 3	Rockingham, N. C.
Saxapahaw	W. L. Holt 3	Graham, N. C.
Seagrove-Love Joy	S. G. Richardson 5	Seagrove, N. C.
Shiloh	Miss Lelia Byerly 4	Lexington, N. C.
Siler City	L. L. Wren 5	Siler City, N. C.
Spencer-China Grove	J. W. Redding *	Spencer, N. C.
Spring Church	Mrs. W. W. Grant 5	Garysburg, N. C.
Tabernacle	T. Worth Trogdon 4	Greensboro, N. C.
Thomasville, Com	C. L. Berrier 2	Thomasville, N. C.
First	D. R. Connell 3	Thomasville, N. C.
Vance	C. A. Wortham 2	Henderson, N. C.
Weaverville	W. G. Edwards 4	Weaverville, N. C.
West Forsyth	J. H. Speas 2	East Bend, N. C.
Whitakers	J. M. Cutchin *	Whitakers, N. C.
Why Not	J. D. Boyles 3	Seagrove, N. C.
Winston-Salem, First	L. P. Burns 1	Winston-Salem, N. C.
Yarborough	W. H. Ballentine 2	Ware Shoals, S. C.

PROCEEDINGS

The 109th session of the North Carolina Annual Conference of the Methodist Protestant Church, was held in the First Methodist Protestant Church, Albemarle, N. C., Rev. C. G. Isley, pastor, beginning on Wednesday, November 4, 1936. The Conference was called to order at 10.00 A. M., with the President, Rev. R. M. Andrews, D.D., in the chair. The Secretary called the roll of ministers, preachers and delegates, after which the following devotional service was entered into, under the direction of the President: Hymn 12, "Come Ye That Love the Lord," was sung, followed by a responsive reading. The President stated that Brother T. A. Williams, a member of the Conference, and Mrs. Geo. L. Reynolds, the wife of one of our pastors, was seriously ill, and asked that they be remembered in prayer. Rev. W. F. Ashburn led in prayer. The Scripture lesson was the 12th chapter of 1st Corinthians. This was followed by the singing of the hymn, "A Charge to Keep I Have."

At 10:45 Conference listened to the Conference sermon preached by Rev. J. Clyde Auman, pastor of Community Church, Thomasville. The subject of the sermon was, "The Middle Wall of Partition," the text: Ephesians 2:14.

At the conclusion of the sermon, Conference stood for the calling of the Roll of the Honored Dead. Before reading, the Secretary asked that the name of Rev. W. F. Kennett, who had passed away during the year, be transferred to the Roll. On motion this was done. The Roll of the Honored dead was then called.

Conference then entered upon the observance of the Lord's Supper. The President was in charge, and was assisted by E. O. Peeler, R. C. Stubbins and T. M. Johnson.

At the close of the communion service a short business session was held. The Conference programs were distributed and adopted subject to such changes as may be necessary. On motion the bar of the Conference was fixed to include the entire auditorium of the church. The Secretary read letters from Brother W. T. Totten, a superannuated minister of this Conference, and from Brother P. E. Bingham, a minister without appointment, each expressing regret that they could not be present at this session.

Rev. W. L. Dorton, pastor of the West Albemarle Baptist Church, was introduced to Conference. On motion Conference adjourned for lunch.

Wednesday Afternoon

1:45. A song service was led by Brother E. Lester Ballard. This was followed by the order of the day—the reading of the President's Message. The Secretary was in the chair while the President read his report. (Report A) At the conclusion of the reading, the message was referred to the Committee on President's Message, and, on motion, the President's official character was passed.

On motion the order of the day—the election of officers—was moved up, and Conference entered upon the order. The President appointed the following tellers: Clyde Payne, O. C. Loy, H. F. Surratt, F. R. Stout. The ballot was distributed for the election of

President. The vote was canvassed and it was announced that Rev. R. M. Andrews, D.D., was elected to succeed himself. On motion of Geo. R. Brown, Conference voted to make the election unanimous.

On motion the Assistant Secretary was instructed to cast the unanimous ballot for the election of C. W. Bates as Secretary. This was done.

On nominations from the floor, the following were elected to succeed themselves in their respective offices: J. H. Allen, Treasurer; J. L. Trollinger, Press Representative; E. G. Cowan, Statistical Secretary; J. Elwood Carroll, Conference Historian; and Paul S. Kennett, Keeper of Records.

The following were elected to constitute the Standing District Committee: J. R. Hutton, J. D. Williams, A. L. Hunter; L. L. Wren, W. C. Goley, J. M. Cutchin.

The Secretary was granted the privilege of selecting his Associate. He announced the appointment of F. W. Paschall to that office.

Ballots were then distributed for the election of the Lay Member of the Stationing Committee. L. L. Wren, delegate from Siler City charge, was declared elected, after a canvass of the vote.

The Secretary made an appeal of an offering for Brother T. A. Williams and his family. The brethren came forward, and when the offering was counted, it was announced that it amounted to $121.00.

The following were elected the Committee on Appeals: J. A. Burgess, J. D. Williams, H. F. Fogleman; L. H. Sides, D. R. Connell, J. F. Williams.

Rev. Geo. W. Haddaway, D.D., Secretary of the Board of Missions, and Mr. Chas. Reiner, Jr., Agent of the Board of Publication at Baltimore, Md., were introduced to Conference.

On motion it was ordered that the Honor Roll credits for World Service be the same as for the past three years.

Conference listened to an address by Dr. G. W. Haddaway, Secretary of the Board of Missions. At the conclusion of the address, Conference adjourned.

Wednesday Night

7:30. The evening service consisted in a review of the Conference Interests. The meeting was presided over by the President of the Conference, and the following brethren spoke: J. E. Pritchard, represented the *Methodist Protestant Herald;* C. W. Bates, the Superannuate Fund; S. W. Taylor, the Board of Church Extension; T. J. Whitehead, the Conference Expense and Conference Debt. After announcements, a motion to adjourn was followed by the closing prayer offered by H. Freo Surratt.

THURSDAY, NOVEMBER 5

9:00. After the singing of a hymn, the Conference roll was called, Conference then entered upon a period of praise and prayer under the direction of C. E. Ridge.

This was followed by a business session. The minutes of yesterday's sessions were read and approved. On motion the secretary was instructed to write a letter of sympathy and fellowship to Brother W. T. Totten.

reports.

President Andrews called attention to a committee suggested in his report last year for the study of a method of apportioning an equitable basis for an enlarged superannuate fund. He appointed the following to bring in recommendations: .J C. Auman, J. C. Madison, R. C. Stubbins, F. R. Stout, J. H. Harkey.

J. B. Trogdon was excused from attendance on this afternoon's session in order that he might attend a funeral.

The report of the Committee appointed to audit the books of J. E. Pritchard, Editor and Business Manager of the *Herald*, was received. (Report B) The Committee to audit the books for the year now closing is J. N. Wills, J. E. Carroll, E. W. Teague.

Rev. Mr. Miller and Rev. Mr. Crammer, both pastors of Methodist Episcopal South churches in Albemarle, were introduced to Conference.

J. E. Pritchard made announcement of the death in Greensboro of Mr. C. F. Coe, brother-in-law of Rev. H. Freo Surratt, a member of this Conference, and one of a long line of Methodist Protestants going back to the beginnings of the denomination in this State. The Secretary was instructed to write Mrs. Coe a letter exressing the sympathy of the Conference in her bereavement. Brothers Surratt, Pritchard and Pittard, were excused until tomorrow afternoon to attend the funeral.

A motion was made that the vote on the overture for Methodist Unification tomorrow be a secret ballot. An amendment was offered to provide that it be a recorded vote. The amendment was voted upon and lost. The original motion was sustained.

The delegate from Seagrove-Love Joy Charge, Brother E. H. Reynolds, was excused from further attendance because of the illness of one of his children.

Conference entered upon a general discussion of the Conference debt, after a statement by the President relative to it. On motion this matter was referred to the Committee on Financial Recommendations.

Dr. Whitely, a pastor of this city, was introduced to Conference.

Chas. Reiner, Jr., Agent at Baltimore of the Board of Publication, addressed the Conference with reference to the various departments of the Book Concern, giving, in the main, an encouraging report of the business.

The Chairman of the Committee on Rural Church, J. W. Braxton, submitted his report. (Report C) On motion the report was adopted. Conference then adjourned.

Thursday Afternoon

1:30. The song service was in charge of E. L. Ballard. Conference then entered upon a business session.

The Committee on Financial Recommendations submitted a partial report. After discussion Conference voted to recommit the report for the inclusion of a financial statement of the debt items.

Mrs. W. C. Hammer, President of the North Carolina Branch of Woman's Work, was introduced and read a report of the year's work.

(Report E)   At the conclusion of the reading, on motion, J. F. Minnis, was loaned to the Board of Missions that he might take up again his work in India.   On motion Brother Minnis was excused from further attendance on this session of Conference.

Rev. C. S. Johnson, D.D., Editor of the Sunday School periodicals, Rev. J. S. Gibbs, Rev. Mr. Honeycut, and Rev. Mr. Weckord, pastors of this city, were introduced.   Atlas Ridge was excused from further attendance on this session of Conference.

On motion Brother J. D. Ross, a lay member of the Asheboro Church, was given the privilege of the floor to make some remarks concerning the balance due on the McCulloch Memorial Fund.   He requested that the present Committee be continued, and that a special effort be made to collect the balance, stating that he wished the Committee to contact the churches and charges which have not yet paid their apportionments, and others if necessary, in order to close the matter by the first of June.   If not paid by then, Brother Ross stated that he wanted to pay the unpaid balance himself.   Brother Ross' requests were granted.

The report of the Committee on Financial Recommendations, which had been recommitted, was again introduced.   On motion the report was adopted. (Report D)

J. A. Burgess, Chairman of the Committee on President's Message, read the report of the Committee, commending the President for his labors, and recommending the adoption of the recommendations and suggestions in the message.

On motion Conference authorized the appointment of a special committee to glean from the reports adopted by this Conference such matters of interest and action as they might find, and keep them before the people through the church paper.   The following constitute the committee: T. J. Whitehead, J. E. Pritchard, J. E. Carroll; D. R. Connell, John Swaim.

Announcements were called for.   The Committee on Pulpit Supply announced the churches to be supplied Sunday by members of Conference.   After the announcement of committee meetings, conference adjourned, prayer being offered by J. C. Auman.

Thursday Night

7:30.   A service of consecration was held at this hour for Rev. J. F. Minnis and his family, who are returning to our India Mission. The service was presided over by Mrs. W. C. Hammer, President of the North Carolina Branch of Woman's Work.   Mrs. J. T. Bowman conducted the devotional service.   A duet was sung by Brothers Reiner and Ballard.   Mrs. Hammer introduced Brother Minnis, who then addressed the Conference on some things he hoped to do on his return to India.   Rev. J. Clyde Auman, a member of the Board of Missions, then presented Brother Minnis and his family for consecration.   The Consecration service was in charge of the President of the Conference.   The benediction was pronounced by F. W. Paschall.   (An offering was taken during the evening to help pay the transportation of the Minnis' car to India.   It amounted to $138.00.)

FRIDAY, NOVEMBER 6

9:00.   Geo. R. Brown was in the chair.   A hymn was sung and the Conference Roll was called.   The service of prayer and praise was led by G. H. Hendry.

Conference entered upon the business session with the President in the chair. The minutes of yesterday's sessions were read and approved. W. D. Reed and Earl A. Cook were excused to attend a funeral.

Geo. R. Brown was in the chair for the order of the day at 10:00 o'clock, which was the hour set aside for the Children's Home. Rev. A. D. Dixon, D.D., Superintendent of the Home, read his report. (Report G) On motion the report was adopted with a rising vote expressing appreciation of the work being done at the Home by Dr. and Mrs. Dixon. Mr. Arch Dixon, the Superintendent of the farm was introduced. Dr. Dixon presented Mrs. E. G. Lowdermilk, the widow of a former Superintendent of the Home.

The following brethren were introduced to Conference: Rev. R. L. Shipley, D.D., Editor of the *Methodist Protestant-Recorder;* Rev. F. L. Gibbs, Secretary of the Department of Religious Education of the Board of Christian Education; Dr. W. A. Parsons, pastor of the Methodist Episcopal Church, Kings Mountain; and Rev. E. W. Fox, pastor of the Methodist Episcopal Church, South, at that place.

Capt. A. M. Rankin, Treasurer of the Children's Home, read his report, which was adopted. (Report H) The report of the Committee on Parsonages was read and adopted. (Report I) The report of the Committee on Ordinances was submitted. On motion it was voted to strike out an objectionable phrase. The report was then adopted. (Report J)

The order of the day at 11:00 was the consideration of High Point College. Dr. G. I. Humphreys, President of the College, was introduced to Conference and read his report. (Report K) It was voted to adopt the report, the Conference standing in an expression of appreciation, and pledge of support.

Conference then entered into a business session. J. H. Trolinger was excused for the afternoon session. The Secretary read letters from Brother A. L. Hunter, one of our superannuated ministers, and from Rev. J. S. Williams, D.D., Chaplain of the Mission of the Good Samaritan, Asheville. A number of the brethren spoke in appreciation of the work Brother Williams is doing. In view of the fact that he is closing his twenty-fifth year as Chaplain of the Mission, it was voted to constitute a committee to make some suitable expression. The committee is as follows: T. M. Johnson, C. W. Bates, J. N. Wills.

The President called attention to an item in a letter from Brother Geo. L. Reynolds, in which he stated that his wife is critically ill in a High Point Hospital. The Secretary was instructed to write Brother Reynolds and convey our sympathy. Also to write Brother G. F. Millaway, and any others who for any reason are absent from this session of Conference. Conference then adjourned for the lunch hour.

Friday Afternoon

1:30. The song service was led by Brother Ballard, after which Conference entered into a business session. On motion Brother T. A. Williams was placed on the superannuated list, and granted an appropriation.

Dr. W. A. Parsons, fraternal messenger from the Blue Ridge-Atlantic Conference of the Methodist Episcopal Church, was presented to Conference, and brought greetings. Dr. James E. Mason; Secretary of Livingstone College, Salisbury, representing the A. M.

E. Zion Church, was introduced, and addressed the Conference. The President responded to these fraternal messages.

The order of the day at 2:30 was to hear the general agents. The following were presented and spoke of their respective departments of the work of the denomination: Rev. Crates S. Johnson, D.D., Editor of the Sunday school periodicals; Rev. R. L. Shipley, D.D., Editor of the *Methodist Protestant-Recorder*; Rev. F. L. Gibbs, Secretary of the Department of Religious Education.

S. W. Taylor was in the chair. Dr. Geo. H. Rhodes, pastor of the First Lutheran Church, Albemarle, was introduced to Conference. The Chairman of the Committee on Church Music, J. W. Braxton, read the report of the Committee. On motion the report was adopted. (Report L) A quartet composed of some of the younger brethren sang two numbers. A motion prevailed that the report of the Committee on Church Music be printed in the *Herald*.

A resolution concerning pastors revisiting former charges was introduced. (Resolution 1) After some discussion a record vote was called for. The resolution passed by a vote of 39 to 29. The report of the Committee on Missions was read and adopted. (Report M)

The following reports were read by Mr. J. Norman Wills, and adopted without discussion: Treasurer of the District Parsonage Trustees, (N); Treasurer of the Superannuated Fund Society, (O); Board of Managers of the Superannuated Fund Society, (P); Trustees of the Roberts Bequest, (Q); Treasurer of the Fuller Bequest, (R).

The report of the Boundary Committee was read and adopted as read. (Report S) The report of the Board of Church Extension was read and adopted. (Report T) The Secretary read a letter from Brother G. F. Millaway, one of our superannuated ministers.

On motion a standing vote of appreciation was given Brothers J. Norman Wills and W. L. Ward for their efficient work on committees and their loyalty to the church. A motion to adjourn prevailed, and conference was dismissed by J. P. Pegg.

Friday Night

7:30. The service was given over to a meeting in the interest of the Laymen's Fellowship in the Conference, the President, Mr. Henry T. Powell, of Henderson, presiding. Mr. W. L. Mann, a lawyer of this city, delivered an address on "The Layman's Point of View."

This address was followed by an address by Dr. W. P. Few, President of Duke University, the fraternal messenger representing the two Conferences of the Methodist Episcopal Church, South, in this State.

At the close of the address, the report of the Nominating Committee was received, and the following officers for the Layman's Fellowship elected: President—F. R. Stout; 1st Vice-President—M. A. Coble; 2nd Vice-President—P. D. Hamilton; Secretary—D. S. Coltrane; Treasurer—J. W. Boyles. The meeting was dismissed with prayer by T. J. Whitehead.

SATURDAY, NOVEMBER 7

9:00. After the singing of a hymn the roll was called. The Conference then entered into the period of prayer and praise, which was in charge of H. W. Bell.

Conference then entered into a business session. The minutes were read, corrected and approved. On motion rule 26 of the Rules of Order was amended to read, "No committee shall meet during the sessions of Conference except by permission." It was voted to strike out items 6 and 7 of the Order of Business. The Secretary was authorized to have the Conference Election Law inserted in the Conference Journal. On motion the report of the Boundary Committee was reconsidered, and Conference voted to refer it to the Committee for amendment. J. L. Amick was seated as delegate from Graham in place of Dr. W. C. Goley.

The order of the day at 10:00 o'clock was to consider the *Methodist Protestant Herald*. The Editor, Dr. J. E. Pritchard, submitted his report. (Report U) The report was adopted with the understanding he would hold it until the end of next week. The chairman of the Committee on *Methodist Protestant Herald*, T. G. Madison, submitted the report of the Committee. (Report V) The report was adopted with a standing vote of appreciation to Dr. Pritchard and to Calvary Church. The President asked all pastors and delegates of charges which have raised subscription and subsidy quotas in full to come forward for recognition.

The report of the Conference Trustees, (Report W), and of the Conference Faculty, (Report X), were presented and adopted. On motion Conference voted to continue the plan for financing the Conference Journal which was adopted by the last—1935—Conference. (See Journal, 1935, page 54.)

The Secretary announced the organization of a Chapter of the Seminary Alumni, and that it has agreed to hypothecate $1,000 of endowment for the Seminary. The officers of the Chapter are: President, C. W. Bates; Vice-President, F. W. Paschall; Secretary-Treasurer, R. A. Hunter.

A letter was read from Brother H. S. B. Thompson, one of our superannuated ministers. J. E. Carroll asked the superannuate relation for Rev. W. D. Reed. Conference granted the request, and authorized the Superannuated Fund Society to grant him an appropriation.

F. W. Paschall, Chairman, submitted the report of the Commission on Evangelism. (Report Y) Because of the approach of the hour of the day, it was voted to make the consideration of the report the order of the day at 2:00 this afternoon.

The order of the day at 11:00 o'clock was the address by the President of the General Conference, Rev. Jas. H. Straughn, D.D., which would be followed by the consideration of the overtures. Dr. Straughn was introduced, as was also Dr. F. W. Stephenson, Secretary of the Board of Christian Education, in charge of colleges.

The Secretary then read the report of the Commission on Methodist Cooperation. On motion the report was adopted. (Report Z) This was followed by the address by Dr. Straughn. At the conclusion of the address, a motion prevailed that when we adjourn for lunch, the first business of the afternoon shall be the consideration of the Plan of Union. Conference then adjourned.

Saturday Afternoon

1:30. The song service was led by E. Lester Ballard. This was followed by the order of the day—the consideration of the overture on the Plan of Union. Dr. Straughn was asked to answer any question which might be in the minds of the members of Conference, and a number of questions were asked.

A motion prevailed that the Secretary read the Overture, and that Conference enter upon a season of prayer before the vote is taken. A telegram of thanks from Mrs. T. A. Williams was read, expressing appreciation of the gift of money sent her by Conference on Friday.

A motion was made by Geo. R. Brown and H. Freo Surratt that the overture on the Plan of Union be adopted. Clyde Payne, J. C. Auman, E. A. Bingham and O. C. Loy, were appointed tellers. On motion the order of the day—consideration of the report of the Committee on Evangelism—was deferred until the vote on the overture shall have been taken. Ballots were distributed, and before voting a number of the brethren offered prayer. The Secretary then began the calling of the roll of ministers and delegates, these coming forward to deposit their ballots. The Secretary announced the result of the ballot as follows:

Number of votes cast	150
Necessary to determine	76
Ministers voting Yes	69
Laymen voting Yes	55
Ministers voting No	8
Laymen voting No	18
Total affirmative vote	124
Total negative vote	26

The President announced that the overture on the Plan of Union had been adopted. Conference was led in prayer by the President of the General Conference. (See Overture No. 1)

Overture No. 2 was then introduced, and on motion adopted. (See Overture No. 2)

Geo. R. Brown was in the chair. The Committee on Official Character was excused for a meeting. Consideration of the report of the Committee on Evangelism was taken up. J. C. Auman spoke to the report emphasizing the Preaching Mission to be held at Raleigh the latter part of this month. On motion the report was adopted, the motion being amended to provide that the report be published in the *Herald* as well as printed in the minutes.

Report AA—the report of the Committee on Pastoral Work, was read by the chairman, S. W. Taylor. The report was adopted without change. The report of the Committee on Religious Education was read and adopted. (Report BB) Dr. F. W. Stephenson, Secretary of the Board of Christian Education, was presented and addressed the Conference.

The final report of the Superannuated Fund Society was read by the Secretary-Treasurer, Mr. J. Norman Wills. . The report was on motion ordered referred for some corrections and additions.

Dr. C. E. Forlines, President of the Westminster Theological Seminary, was introduced and addressed the Conference on some of the needs of that institution. He made two suggestions: 1. That an offering be taken in the churches and Sunday schools for the Seminary. 2. That the Conference appropriate $100 for the support of the Extension School held by the Seminary at High Point College during the summer.

G. L. Curry introduced a resolution, (Resolution 2), concerning the Conference relation to the Seminary and the Extension Course.

7:30. After the singing of a hymn, Conference entered into a business session. By common consent the report of the Treasurer of the Conference for the year 1934-35, which was received too late to be included in the printed minutes, was ordered printed in this year's Journal.

The report of the Secretary-Treasurer of the Board of Education was read and adopted. (Report CC) The report of the meeting of the laymen held on Friday was on motion ordered printed in the Journal.

A resolution was introduced by S. W. Taylor concerning the time for the holding of the Annual Conference sessions: to begin on Wednesday and conclude on Sunday night. An amendment was offered to begin on Thursday and conclude on Monday. The amendment carried and the resolution as amended was adopted. (Resolution 3)

On motion the resolution concerning the Seminary Extension course was taken up. It was moved to consider by items. Items 1, 2, and 3 were adopted. Item 4, concerning an appropriation of $100.00 was ordered stricken from the resolution. The resolution was adopted. (An effort was then made to raise the $100 by securing cash and pledges to under-write it. $75.00 was raised, and the balance secured later. Secretary)

Conference voted to recommend Brother Sulon Gurney Ferree, a student in Westminster Theological Seminary, to the Board of Christian Education for aid.

The report of the Committee on Superannuates was submitted. After considerable discussion it was voted to defer final action until Monday, in the meantime to have the report mimeographed. Consideration of the report was made the order of the day at 9:30 Monday.

At the request of Dr. Stephenson, the Committee on Religious Education was asked to insert a recommendation in their report that a Committee of Five be set up in the Conference to work with the denominational Board of Religious Education. Conference then adjourned.

SUNDAY, NOVEMBER 8

11:00. At this hour Conference listened to the ordination sermon preached by Rev. C. E. Forlines, D.D., LL.D., President of Westminster Theological Seminary, and a member of this Conference. The subject of the sermon was: "The Functions of the Christian Ministry." The text: 1 Cor. 12:28. Following the sermon, William Miller Howard, Jr., was ordained to eldership in the Church of Christ. The presbytery was composed of the President of the Conference assisted by Geo. R. Brown and T. M. Johnson.

2:30. This hour was set aside for a memorial service honoring Rev. W. F. Kennett. An obituary was read by Dr. J. E. Pritchard.

An offering was taken for the superannuates, which amounted to $27.50.

7:30. The service was in the nature of a rally in the interest of the Board of Christian Education. The President of the Conference Council, T. J. Whitehead, presided. The speaker was Dr. P. E. Lindley, Dean of High Point College. The subject of the address: "The Church's Responsibility for Its Community."

MONDAY, NOVEMBER 9

9:30. After the singing of a hymn and the calling of the roll Conference entered into the period of prayer and praise under the direction of C. L. Spencer.

The order of the day at 9:30 was the consideration of the report of the special Committee on Superannuate Funds. Consideration was deferred until the minutes could be read, and other matters attended to. J. E. Garlington was received into membership in this Conference by transfer from the Louisiana Conference. On motion W. M. Howard, Jr., who was ordained on yesterday, was received into membership. On motion the Conference Treasurer was authorized to reimburse Dr. Forlines for his expenses from and to Westminster.

The report of the special committee was then taken up. (Report FF) An amendment was offered changing the basis and amount of assessment. The report as amended was adopted.

The report of the Committee on Social Service was adopted. (Report GG) The Committee on Life Insurance for Ministers submitted a report which was adopted. (Report HH) On motion J. Clyde Auman was asked to furnish a copy of the Conference sermon for publication in the *Methodist Protestant Herald*.

The Committee to make suitable recognition of Brother J. S. Williams' services as Chaplain of the Mission of the Good Samaritan, Asheville, introduced resolutions which were adopted. (Report II) The report of the Executive Committee of the Conference Council of Religious Education was submitted and adopted as read. (Report JJ) It was ordered that the financial statement of the Treasurer of the Council be included in the report.

The report of the Boundary Committee was resubmitted. The report was adopted as revised. The report of the Committee on Stewardship was adopted as read. (Report KK) The Expense Account of the Conference Secretary was accepted. (Report LL) The report of the Statistical Secretary was ordered printed in the Conference Journal without reading. (Report MM) The report of the Committee on Official Character was read. The chairman of the Committee, T. M. Johnson, spoke to the report. The report was adopted. (Report NN) An offering was taken for the janitor which amounted to $13.75.

The Conference Treasurer, Mr. J. H. Allen, submitted a tentative report. He was given the privilege of submitting the report to the Secretary after the adjournment of Conference for inclusion in the Journal. (Report OO) The Nominating Committee submitted its report. On motion the report was adopted. (Report PP)

Invitations were received for place for holding the next session of Conference. Asheboro Church and Tabernacle Church extended invitations. Conference voted to meet with the Asheboro Church.

The pastor of Tabernacle Church was asked to extend thanks to his congregation for their invitation.

The report of the Committee on Fraternal Relations was submitted and on motion adopted. (Report QQ) The Conference Faculty submitted a suplimental report which was adopted. The Secretary of Conference was asked to write Rev. A. L. Hunter and his son, Rev. R. A., a letter of sympathy in the serious illness of wife and mother.

The report of the Stationing Committee was called for. It was held in abeyance for some other matters. The report of the Committee on Conference Program was submitted and adopted. (Report SS) On motion it was voted to hold the next session of Conference beginning Thursday, November 4, 1937. Dr. Straughn spoke briefly expressing his pleasure at being permitted to attend this session of our Conference.

The report of the Stationing Committee (Report RR) was then read. President Andrews asked that after adjournment all who would to come forward and pledge to do their best during the coming year. He then led the Conference in the closing prayer, and Conference stood adjourned.

R. M. ANDREWS, President,

C. W. BATES, Secretary.

Albemarle, N. C.
November 9, 1936.

REPORTS

(A) THE PRESIDENT'S REPORT

To the North Carolina Conference of the Methodist Protestant Church, in First Church, Albemarle, November 4, 1936, in the one hundred and ninth session;

My Dear Brethren:

It is with a profound sense of gratitude to our Heavenly Father who has brought us to this glad hour that we enter upon the duties of this conference today. We are doing it with a consciousness that others have labored and we are entering upon their labors and that without them our work can not be well done. We also know something of the joy they had as they engaged in the activities of the conference sessions aforetimes, and think that if it's possible for them to do it, they are very near us now with a tremendous concern that we shall be faithful and do well our part. Let us pray much that we shall be true to the tasks to which we are called and shall faithfully follow in their train.

We have found it most difficult in making out this report to properly appraise all the work our churches have done this year. So much of it is routine and as all routine is a continuation of what has gone on before, without regard to its excellence or commonplaceness, it is quite easy for one to overlook the value of the routine of the commonplace. For although it is worth while that we keep the church open, that the services be regularly held and that the routine work be kept going, such matters do not get into our reports and may therefore appear to be of no value. But they are most vital to the existence of the church, although they have no part in our records. We have scanned the reports of pastors and delegates in our hands to discover signs of progress, signs of improvement, and now present some of them to you. We are presenting them in kaledioscopic fashion to save your time and the space in the Conference Journal.

New Buildings

Our people at Fallston have erected a beautiful and most commodious church building to replace the old. Mills Grove is engaged in the erection of a new building to replace the church; likewise Spring Church. This building is to take the place of one destroyed by storm this year. Mt. Pleasant Church, Mt. Pleasant Charge, has erected a hut, additional Sunday school rooms have been built for Baltimore Church on West Forsyth Charge, and Pine Bluff Church, Midland Church, and plans are completed for new Sunday school rooms have been made at Shiloh and Bethany Church, Randolph Charge. Welch Memorial, High Point, completed a church hut this year; Midway Church is preparing to build one. The pastor of Shiloh Church, Shiloh Charge, is enjoying a splendid new parsonage. First Church, Charlotte, has added to their tabernacle, and numerous churches and parsonages have been repaired and improved this year.

Both High Point College and the Children's Home have been the beneficiaries of the bequest of Mr. and Mrs. A. S. Pickett. This amount when fully paid will most likely enable Superintendent Dixon to pay off all debts on the Home and will enable President Humphreys to furnish the new library building which is now being erected at· High Point College.

We are delighted to state that some of our churches which have been burdened with debts are now paying them off. While it must of necessity be a slow process with many because the debts are large, we are hoping that ere long all these debts will be paid, and the deeds of trust or mortgages which have been such a source of worry to our leaders will soon be consumed in smoke and ashes, to the glory of God and the delight of many congregations.

We find here and there a change of attitude towards the church. Some who have been under the juniper tree or in the Slough of Despond, greatly to the hindrance of the cause of Christ, are showing signs of new life and we believe, if their improvement continues, we shall see them in the workers groups where they used to delight to be. For no one can do much while discouraged except complain of his sorry lot and declares that it is futile to attempt to change conditions however bad they may be.

Of course there are still those with us who have grown an intellectual and a spiritual epidermis too thick to be punctured by the arrows of truth or moved by the appeals of world need. To them salvation is purely a local matter. The only gospel they believe in is one of self preservation, which in its practice excludes all others. They heed not the command of our Lord, "Go ye into all the world and preach the gospel to every creature"—it certainly has no place in their purpose. It is an anomolus condition for a church to call itself a Christian church and all the while fail to observe the one principal which makes it Christian—that of being missionary. Lest you fail to grasp what I mean, it is this, we are doing entirely too little for world redemption. I doubt that we are doing too much for ourselves; but we are doing entirely too little for the benevolent, missionary and educational enterprises of our denomination. We must increase our acceptances for World Service and must pay them. While 28 ·pastors reported all claims paid out of a total of 70 reporting to me,—and this is good—we should set for our goal for next year a larger increase of churches which pay all claims. The money is needed for our conference claims and for our denominational activities outside the North Carolina Conference. Let's pay our pastors more! Some ten or a dozen charges are promising an increased salary for next year. Three churches report a decrease. While disclaiming any thought that the support of the pastor is the major project of any church, he certainly ought to be supported. Not to live in luxury, but surely to live so he can give his entire thought and time to the ministry to which he is called. It ought not to be necessary in these days, under the proper arrangements made for pastoral support, for a pastor of a charge to be compelled to labor for his support outside his pastorate. I mean, he should not have to leave his church during the week to supplement his support.

The Need of System

There are, I suppose, just a few churches in our entire conference which have a working system in raising their finances. Just why so many otherwise reasonable men and women shy at a system for raising the money necessary to pay their pastors and the Conference claims, I have failed to understand. We have pastoral charges the per capita contribution to all claims of which is two dollars; others pay fifteen times that amount, or thirty dollars, and the difference in the per capita contributions in all cases can be traced to the lack of system; of the use per capita contributions when compared to other denominations. It surely is not because we are poorer than most of them. The reason must be found elsewhere, and we trace it to the lack of proper methods in raising our claims. Presupposing that our members are regenerated when they join our church, and that the pastor has properly impressed upon them when they join that they are pledging to it their financial support, we are persuaded that a properly organized and wisely worked financial plan in our churches would secure larger contributions to all claims. There is absolutely no substitute for it.

Methodist Union

We have discovered much ignorance about this plan of unification. It is not the purpose of this paragraph to attempt to enlighten the unenlightened, but we do want to emphasize a few things. First, acquaint yourself with the plan. Make a sincere effort to understand it and to evaluate properly its implications. Second, when you have made up your opinion to oppose it, do it as a Christian. If you think it is wrong, say so, and oppose it as being wrong. But if a majority of your brethren and sisters favor it and you just cannot go into the new church, then for goodness sake, don't be a "bull in a china shop," and try to destroy all that's worth while in the church because a majority of the churches do not agree with you. Third, if the overture is adopted by the participating denominations, and union is surely in the offing, please do not sit down and wait for the coming day. Be diligent, be faithful, be careful, that the cause of the Kingdom of Heaven shall not suffer. There has not come to us a greater challenge since the days our forefathers went out to build a new church, and we cannot be true children of those heroic sires if we fail to make the most possible out of this opportunity just ahead. The plan will be presented by Dr. Straughn and sufficient time will be given to its consideration at that period.

Building a Conference Program

Any one who attends the sessions of our Conference and listens to the excellent reports adopted by our hearty approval might feel that surely something worth while will be started now.' But after the printer is done with those reports it to often happens all others are likewise through with them. True they are in the Conference Journal and may be read by any one who desires to refresh his mind about the acts of the Conference, but we must get more out of them than that. So we are proposing that a committee be constituted by this Conference to select from the reports of the committee reporting to it such items, recommendations, paragraphs, etc., which may be used in building a conference program for the coming year, and that the report of this committee when adopted by the Conference shall become by virtue of this fact our program for the year.

Evangelism

Whatever other affairs a Christian church may be engaged in, and however important these may appear to be, there is nothing more vital to the life of the church than soul saving; and surely no sincere follower of Christ wants to miss the opportunity of bringing men to Christ; yet we have churches in which few or no conversions are reported in an entire year. We know that some of our churches are located where it would be most difficult to make much increase in membership. Still evangelism is a spirit thrilled with great zeal for the cause of Christ, and Philip exhibited·it in a desert place. None of us ought to be without it wherever we be and whatever we are engaged in. It is this spirit in the church which wins men to Christ. So however efficient we may be in all of the activities of the kingdom, the spirit which motivates every act of ours should be one of love for Christ and for the lost world for which He died.

Official Acts

November 13th—E. P. Hamilton, a student in High Point College was appointed supply pastor of Mt. Zion Charge.

November 13th—Accepted the resignation of W. D. Reed as pastor of Porter Church and appointed C. G. Isley pastor instead.

November 13th—Released W. M. Loy from Halifax Charge as its pastor for the year, and later assigned him to Fountain Place, Burlington.

November 16th—Appointed W. C. Clark as supply pastor of Democrat Charge.

November 18th—Appointed J. E. Carroll pastor of Shady Grove Church.

November 27th—Leo Pittard a student in High Point College was appointed supply pastor of the church at Brown Summit.

November 22nd—A delegation representing the members of Love's Grove Church visited me and requested that their church be served by another pastor than the one appointed to serve Midland Charge. After explaining to them that unless the present pastor should resign or he should be convicted of some offense requiring his removal, I had no authority to change him. The pastor upon learning of the dissatisfaction of some of the people at Love's Grove offered his resignation to me, which was accepted and at the request of the same group of members W. D. Reed was appointed to serve the church for the remainder of the year.

December 8th—J. E. Garlington, a student in High Point College was appointed supply pastor of Midway Church on the Greensboro road.

December 9th—The Standing District Committee met with me and accepted the invitation of First Church, Albemarle, to hold the present session of the conference there. The invitation was accepted with pleasure.

December 14th—I held a conference with a group of the members of Halifax Charge to make arrangements for pastoral supply until a regular pastor could be secured.

December 19th—In company with two ministerial students at High Point College, I visited a group of churches in the South Carolina Conference as a friendly messenger, and held conference with some of their laymen relative to supplying a few of their churches with student pastors from High Point College; but because of the distance and poor bus schedules we decided nothing could be done.

This trip was taken in compliance with conference action last year. We left them with full assurance of our wish to aid them and of our love for them.

Our Chase City Church—Being unable to secure a pastor for this church from among our own men who live nearest it, a request was made by the officials of that church that Rev. George W. M. Taylor, pastor of the Methodist Episcopal Church, South, of Chase City, be permitted to preach for them this year. The request was granted and he held regular services there until he was transferred last month to another charge. I arranged for and held several group meetings of the members of various churches this year and although the attendance was never very large the interest was gratifying and we believe the plan may be worked to the greater benefit of many of our churches.

May 8th—A congregational meeting of the members of Moriah Church was held to which the resignation of W. M. Howard as pastor was presented. Following this meeting he was appointed pastor of Halifax Charge.

May 20-27 Inclusive—I attended the sessions of the General Conference held in First Church, High Point.

Besides the foregoing I have held many quarterly conferences, attended several meetings as a trustee or member of boards, and attended all the meetings of the Pastors' Federation held in the Conference.

Dedicated the educational rooms of Friendship Church and the Hollister Church, which although erected years ago was dedicated this year. Represented our church on the Council of the Rural Church at Duke University in three meetings during the year.

Our Superannuates

More and more I am made aware of the inadequate assistance this Conference in giving to our superannuated preachers and their wives. So little is done that we must feel ashamed to publish the amounts. I do not think we need to expect a large increase to this cause with our present method. We hope that this Conference may do something or prepare to do something to more fully express our appreciation of the services of these fathers in Israel.

Deceased

Rev. W. F. Kennett was called to his eternal home January 14th, this year. His was a long life of service and the memory of his faithfulness will abide with us through the years. The following brethren were appointed to prepare an obituary which will be read at the proper time to this Conference: J. E. Pritchard, W. F. Ashburn, J. N. Wills.

Budget Schedule

We would like to see continued the schedule adopted by last conference for raising the annual conference claims, which is as follows:

January-February, A. C. expenses.
March-April, High Point College.
May-June, Church Extension.

July-August, Annual Conference debt.

September-October, Superannuates.

That September and October be tithing months for members of our church who do not practice tithing regularly.

Conclusion

There are other matters of vital concern which have a right to go into this report, but I withhold them because I have emphasized most of them in my weekly letters in the *Herald*. I have greatly enjoyed the work, although I was prevented from making a few appointments because of sickness. I shall ever remember the uniform courtesy and kindness received from all our pastors. We have enjoyed the hospitality of your homes and the fellowship of your spirit. And now may the grace of our Lord and Saviour Jesus Christ be with you all. Amen.

Respectfully submitted,

R. M. ANDREWS, President.

(B) REPORT OF THE COMMITTEE APPOINTED TO AUDIT THE BOOKS OF THE METHODIST PROTESTANT HERALD

In obedience to the request of Dr. Pritchard made to the last Annual Conference, and in conformity to the Conference action, we have examined the books of the *Methodist Protestant Herald* and find them to be in excellent condition. A simple, but complete system of book-keeping has been installed, giving an accurate and satisfactory record of receipts, disbursements, and other items which are necessary for the information of the editor, and all others interested. We have not made a detailed audit of all the items, as we did not regard it as necessary. We commend Dr. Pritchard, and his able accountant, Miss Mary C. McCulloch, for the efficient manner in which the books are kept.

J. NORMAN WILLS,
J. R. HUTTON,
E. W. TEAGUE.

(C) REPORT OF THE COMMITTEE ON RURAL CHURCH

The Committee on Rural Church has tried, in a small way, to ascertain what is being done to improve both the physical appearance and the efficiency of the rural church in North Carolina. The Committee has found that progress is being made, and is very noticeable when viewed over a period of ten or twenty years.

The Committee wishes to commend those pastors and churches which have made improvements in the worship service and in the appearance and comfort of the church in which they worship. There were a few who reported to the Committee that improvements had been, or were in the process of being made; while there are many other improvements which are noticeable that have not been reported.

However, while many improvements have been made, there is room for development and improvement in all of our rural churches.

The Committee, therefore, is offering suggestions which it hopes, if taken, will help solve two of the outstanding problems which the rural church is facing today. The two problems are the same as the two which the Committee offered suggestions for last year, namely: (1) The improvement of the appearance and comfort of the physical equipment of the church, and (2) The development of a more adequate worship program.

The Committee feels that the most attractive place in any community should not be some filling station or cross-road store, although we like for these to be pleasing to the eye, but the most attractive place should be the church, which stands for Beauty and Purity. We suggest therefore,

1. That the church grounds be beautified by planting shrubbery and sowing grass seed and cleaning up unattractive places near the church.

2. That more attention be given to the appearance and comfort of the church building, such as:

    a. Keeping the building swept, cleaned and dusted.

    b. Keeping the building well repaired and painted.

    c. Seeing that all broken window panes are replaced.

    d. Seeing that the floor has a carpet of some kind, especially along the aisles.

    e. Seeing that living flowers are provided for each service.

We suggest that someone be appointed in each Conference district to try to create an interest in and encourage church beautification. This interest may be created by putting on a contest between the various churches in the district for beautification. The committee suggests that all improvements be reported to the chairman of the Rural Church Committee in order that the same may be reported through the *Herald* by him at various times.

Another noticeable need of many rural churches is that of a more adequate, or better, worship program. This Committee realizes that neither it, nor any person, cannot guarantee a worship experience at any given time, or by any given formula. But we feel that there are certain conditions under which a person is more likely to worship than others. We therefore, offer two orders of service for your consideration, or for those who may not have a better order:

Number 1

Prelude—(Instrumental, if possible. A hymn may be played for the prelude if desired.)

Call to Worship—(We suggest that the minister use, some appropriate verse of Scripture for this. He may have the congregation respond if practicable.)

Hymn—

Responsive Reading—

Gloria Patri—

Prayer—

Announcements—

Offering—

Offertory—(We suggest quiet music for this.)

Prayer—
Scripture Reading—
Announcements—
Offering—
Hymn—
Sermon—
Prayer—
Hymn—
Benediction—

We find that where churches have been having afternoon services, in order to have more preaching services, that they do not, generally, measure up to the morning service in quality, or effectiveness. We therefore, suggest that where two churches are near enough to enable the pastor to drive from one to the other in fifteen or twenty minutes that you consider the possibility of preaching at one church at 10 o'clock, and let the Sunday school follow the preaching service, while the pastor goes to the other church for a service at 11:15 o'clock, or as near that as possible. This has worked well at some churches.

The Committee.

(D)   REPORT OF COMMISSION ON FINANCIAL RECOMMENDATIONS

Your Committee on Financial Recommendations submits the following report:

1. We recommend that the items of the budget remain the same as last year, namely:

Annual Conference Expenses:

President's Salary	$2,250.00
President's travel expenses and office help	500.00
Secretary's Salary	100.00
Treasurer's Salary	100.00
Statistician's Salary	25.00
Press Agent's Salary	25.00

Incidentals	150.00	
Herald Subsidy	200.00	
		$3,350.00

Superannuate Fund	2,500.00
Church Extension	2,000.00
Annual Conference Debt	2,000.00
High Point College	5,000.00

2. We recommend that the District Parsonage Trustees be instructed to sell the Greensboro parsonage as soon as a reasonable price can be secured, and that the funds realized thereon be applied on the indebtedness of the Parsonage Trustees.

3. Realizing that the amount of money raised for World Service is very small in comparison with the amount requested by the General Conference, we recommend that the pastors and members place more stress on this item during the coming year.

4. We recommend that the churches post a list of tithers and regular contributors in some appropriate place in the church, but that the amounts be not included.

R. M. ANDREWS,
T. J. WHITEHEAD.

(E) REPORT OF THE NORTH CAROLINA BRANCH OF WOMEN'S WORK

The missionary enterprise has come to the "open door" of a new age, in which new and strange forces are playing a momentous part, and challenging the fundamentals of historic Christianity. A study of church history makes plain that in world affairs, in which we find ourselves today, whenever and wherever the missionary spirit has been manifested moral advance has been registered and human well being made secure. What the church needs to meet this world situation is a new baptism of the missionary spirit. The North Carolina Branch of Women's Work, sensing this great need, has put forth strenuous effort to assist the church in putting on a program, which will meet the needs of the hour. During the conference year just closing, we can report advance along the line of interest and activity, but financially practically the same as last year, the total amount being

Disbursements

General Conference Treasurer	$4,701.48
High Point College	791.35
Children's Home	1,514.22
Bethel Home	510.17
High Point College Student Loan Fund	498.38
Methodist Protestant Herald	100.00
Contingent Fund	150.00
China Car	275.00
	$8,540.60

Numerically—Of the approximately 30,000 Methodist Protestants in North Carolina there are 12,000 women. Only about one-third of them are in the organizations of women's work, which includes the auxiliaries and Aid Societies. The State has been divided into eighteen districts, each corresponding to the Conference Districts, and with Mrs. H. C. Nicholson, chairman, capable leader that she is, and with her cooperating district chairmen, the work is promising.

Without a word or intimation of criticism: if the pastors and delegates present would lend their wholehearted support to this phase of church work, mountains would become mole hills and the entire denomination would see the result of labors along this line. Churches which have active, thoroughly organized women's auxiliaries are those which have made greatest progress. Only one-sixth of the womanhood of the North Carolina Conference is a small percentage, but that small number is unexcelled in capability and willingness. In many of the rural churches there are not sufficient numbers to fill suggested secretarial offices, and in these cases there could be a merging of offices.

Departments—(Missionary Education)

Two special projects have been used this year: A Missionary Catechism on our own denominational work, mimeographed and mailed monthly by the secretary of missionary education to each auxiliary, and a Travelogue of our Home Mission fields given with slides by Rev. E. L. Ballard. These can be given in rural as well as city churches.

Two of the Districts in their meetings threw out challenges, District No. 5 recommending a campaign or crusade for church attendance. This was adopted by the executive committee and Mrs. E. L. Ballard was named chairman of a committee to put on the same. District No. 2 was the first to respond to the call to raise $200 for the India equipment fund, and challenged other districts to do their part.

Other districts have unitedly used the study books, cooperated in the "Summer Special," which was contributions for the car for our missionaries in China, the amount of which was more than $275.00.

Thank Offering—While our Thank Offering financial goal was not reached on account of bad weather, or failure to get program material sufficiently early, the educational value of these services was appreciable. Accentuation of Christian Education at the fall Thank Offering and of Missions at the February Thank Offering services is customary.

Literature—North Carolina has had the distinction of leading all Branches in *Missionary Record* subscriptions. This is probably attributable to the custom of sending free subscriptions to newly organized auxiliaries. The Secretary of Literature reports an increase of monthly program leaflets distributed to auxiliaries and of orders for year books and study books.

Spiritual Life—There is a general tendency to stress more than ever the spiritual life of the auxiliaries. The Secretary has been actively and energetically urging the use of the Guide Books, which contain complete programs.

Temperance and Christian Citizenship—Many of the auxiliaries observed October as Temperance and Christian Citizenship month, giving interesting and worthwhile programs. The Secretary urges the use of the Silver and Gold Medal Contest as a means of interesting the young people.

Young People's Work—There is much interest manifested in the young people of our church under the leadership of our enthusiastic secretary, who has joined in the worldwide Youth Movement. Outstanding in this phase of the department is the monthly publication of a Youth Bulletin.

Pastors' Aid Secretary—The creation of the office of Pastors' Aid Secretary provides for work formerly done by the Ladies' Aid Societies. In this way the auxiliaries are not neglecting any part of the local church work and report more than $10,000 raised for debts paid, repairs on churches and parsonages during the year.

Student Loan Fund—High Point College Student Loan Fund meets a great need. Twenty-three students were helped during the last College year by loans, not exceeding $100 each.

Benevolences—It is impossible to enumerate the benefits derived from gifts to the Children's Home, Bethel Home, and various phases of welfare work.

The women of the North Carolina Branch of Women's Work have never failed in their loyalty to the general program of our denomination and pledge their continual allegiance.

MRS. W. C. HAMMER, President.

(F)   REPORT OF THE COMMITTEE ON THE PRESIDENT'S MESSAGE

The untiring efforts of our president during the past year, as indicated by his report, merit the sincere appreciation of every member of this Conference. We believe that his diligence in service has been paralleled by his saneness of procedure in handling the affairs of the church and its program.

We have carefully studied the President's Message and make the following report and recommendations:

1. That this message be printed in full in the Conference Journal, and that the principal items of this report be presented to the people of the local churches by the different pastors throughout the Conference.

2. We refer the paragraph on system in finances to the Committee on Stewardship.

3. The item on church union is very timely and we heartily endorse it.

4. That we concur in the President's suggestions for building a conference program and recommend that the President be empowered to appoint the committee called for. (See report)

5. The discussion of evangelism touches the very heart of the Christian purpose and program. We call the attention of the Committee on Evangelism to this paragraph, and urge that committee to study the possibilities of our cooperating with the program of the National Preaching Mission in a statewide or conferencewide evangelistic effort.

6. We recognize the utter inadequacy of conference assistance of superannuates, and we look to the recommendations of the special committee appointed to study this problem.

7. We favor the President's suggestion in regard to the continuation of the schedule adopted last conference for the raising of Annual Conference claims. (See report)

Respectfully submitted,

J. A. BURGESS, Chairman,
F. R. STOUT,
N. G. BETHEA,
J. C. MADISON,
J. M. MORGAN,
DR. J. SWAIM,
F. D. HAMILTON,
O. G. CARPENTER,
C. C. ROBBINS.

(G) REPORT OF THE SUPERINTENDENT OF THE CHILDREN'S HOME

Albemarle, N. C., November 6, 1936

Dear Fellow Workers:

With gratitude to God for His wonderful guidance, and to His people for their splendid help in the work of this Home for another year, we take pleasure in presenting to you our annual report, which shows progress.

The Children

It is of the children you wish to hear first; for whatever else is done in connection with this work, it is all done for the children. We now have 111 children, all of whom are in school except two little boys and two little girls who are too young, and two boys who will soon be going out. So every school morning 105 boys and girls leave our doors with lunch and books in hand to attend school. They rank well in school with the other children of the community, and both our boys and girls take high rank on the athletic fields. One teacher said to us in a note, "I note that all your children have a very high sense of fair play on the athletic fields."

The doctors and the dentists in High Point have been universal in their kindness in rendering services to us in the Home without cost.

The health of the children has been unusually good. No serious illness has come upon us. A recent broken bone, and an operation for appendicitis are among the most serious afflictions we have had. These are both doing well.

With few exceptions we have a very fine group of children. There is real joy in living with them and in working for them. In a group this large there are always some problem children, and a problem child frequently upsets several others, so there is scarcely a day goes by that there is not some problem to be settled. We try to settle these problems in the fear of the Lord and for the good of the child. Some of the problems are serious ones for the child concerned, and also for a larger group who are affected, or who may be affected by the problem. These cases take weeks and sometimes months to settle; but we have tried to solve them without burdening you with a recital of the details of those problems.

Dr. T. M. Johnson once said: "No man cares for the chips and shavings of your workshop. He wants to see what you have produced." In a similar manner we have felt that you do not care for a recital of the accomplishments of the Home year by year. Is the Home paying dividends on the annual investments? That is your concern.

That we may get a glimpse of some of the accomplishments of this Home during the last eight years we are giving under the next heading some of the outstanding facts.

A Contrast·

Some weeks ago some one of the agencies gathering facts about child-caring institutions asked us to answer a lot of questions giving contrasts which would show whether the institution was really going forward or not, and the following facts are about what we told them. The comparison is drawn between our condition in October, 1928, and October, 1936. The facts are as follows:

1. In 1928, we had only three old mules, which gave completely out the next summer. Now, we have five good mules and one young mare.

2. In 1928 we had 11 cows and no young cattle. Now we have 15 good cows and 15 head of young cattle.

3. In 1928, no tractor; now, a good caterpillar tractor.

4. In 1928, no wagon; now, two good two-horse wagons.

5. In 1928, two automobiles which soon had to be junked; now, one good automobile and one that is about gone.

6. In 1928, about 30 chickens; now, 332 chickens.

7. In 1928, one dilapidated chicken house; now, two good chicken houses.

8. In 1928, almost no farming tools; now, a fair lot of farming tools.

9. In 1928, very little hay and no ensilage; now, plenty of hay for the winter, and about 48 tons of ensilage.

10. In 1928, almost no supplies in storage rooms; now, well stocked storage rooms.

11. In 1928, poor fences. Now, poor fences; we have patched the fences as long as we can. It will cost quite a bit to put fences in order during next year. We need posts.

12. In 1928, one old Ford bus; now, one old International bus.

13. In 1928, nearly all double beds; now, all single beds.

14. In 1928, worn and splintered pine floors in girls' dormitory. Now, oak floors over all pine floors in girls' dormitory except in the chapel.

15. In 1928, old furnaces; now, a new furnace under each dormitory.

16. In 1928, old ranges in the kitchens; now, a new Majestic range in the girls' dormitory; boys' dormitory must have one soon.

17. In 1928, no refrigerators. Now, two large refrigerators and a drinking fountain; the three cost $1,375, paid for with coupons.

18. In 1928, no separate home for the superintendent's family. Now, a good home for the superintendent's family, with enlarged and beautiful campus. Nearly all the shrubbery was donated.

19. In 1928, no family laundry building. Now, a new laundry building, and all our heavy laundry to be done for five years for the use of the building.

20. In 1928, all children except high school pupils were taught by two teachers in the Home. Each child who was old enough would go to school half a day and work half a day. Now, all children of school age attend the Jamestown school, and remain in school all day. The state and county furnish the bus for transportation.

21. In 1928, only 72 children in the Home; now, 111 children in the Home.

22. In 1928, no child of the Home had ever graduated from high school. Now, 15 have graduated from high school, 5 have graduated from a business school, two have graduated from High Point College, three others have attended college for three years, and two have gone to college for two years; one has graduated as a trained nurse.

We are truly proud of the most of these who have pressed on beyond the high school work. It is only the occasional child we get here who cannot be developed into noble manhood or womanhood, and if some plan could be developed whereby such ones might be weeded out, then those left would do better still.

We found 72 children here; 79 have gone out since we came, and we still have 111. So we have handled for the church 190 children in these eight years. What the results are and will be eternity alone will reveal.

Clothing for the Children

The children must be clothed for home, for school, and for church and Sunday school, and of course for party and commencement occasions like other children. We try to clothe them as cheaply as possible, and yet they must not be put to shame when they go out to mingle with others of their ages.

Mrs. Dixon has done an abundance of corresponding this fall relative to clothing for the children. She has succeeded in getting women's organizations somewhere to furnish winter outfits for nearly all the girls, and for several of the boys. Somehow it is easier to get clothing for girls than for boys. We mean to keep trying for the boys.

The Farm

It has been most difficult to farm this season. Really the most difficult season we have had during the eight years. The farmers and the boys have worked harder than usual, and to their encouragement the farm produce only fell a little short of that of last year.

The farm produced 3,636 pounds of pork, 1,581 pounds of beef, 369 chickens for the tables, 113 bushels of Irish potatoes, 270 bushels of sweet potatoes, 12,802 gallons of milk, 1,858 dozen eggs, 115 loads of hay, 436 bushels of wheat, 36 bushels of oats and barley, with straw from the grain, 3,600 bunches of top fodder, 358 gallons of molasses, 100 or more bushels of cane seed, 48 tons of ensilage, and food from garden and truck patches estimated at $500. This amount of produce at most conservative prices, with a cash item of $52.50, amounts to a total of $8,369.52.

Live Stock

We have 5 mules, 1 young mare, 15 milk cows and 15 head of young cattle, 1 bull, 3 stock hogs, 18 hogs for killing, 4 shoats, and 332 chickens on the yard. These are worth at least $2,500. They could not be replaced for that.

How Financed

Last May we said, in part, to the General Conference: "The Home is inadequately financed, and yet we have fed the children sufficiently, and have clothed them so that they are not ashamed anywhere. When our youngsters are mingling with the crowd we challenge you to pick them out and designate the orphan child from the community child. The mark of institutional life is not upon them. Occasionally we get a bequest, and we trust that more and more of them will come. These bequests have proven great blessings to the Home.

"With the present number of children, it takes $1,665 per month to run the Home, counting 55½ cents per day per child. This comes from the following sources:

The General Conference, per year..$1,600.00
The Duke Endowment (1935)... 1,947.69
The N. C. Branch, Woman's Auxiliary, per year, about........... 1,500.00
The 25th Anniversary Offering.. 3,016.70
Thanksgiving and Christmas... 2,591.03

"The entire income for 1935 was $20,742.41, and that means that Sunday schools and churches and individuals of North Carolina Annual Conference contributed for the Home, above their share in the Anniversary and Thanksgiving and Christmas offerings, the total of $10,687.01. You can readily see that the great task of the management of the Homes is to devise ways and means by which the money may be raised and the monthly bills met."

Based upon this statement, Mrs. D. S. Coltrane made a motion and led the discussion which succeeded in getting the General Conferece to amend the Finance Committee's report, and grant the Home $400 more per year for the quadrennium.

Bequest

Several bequests have come our way recently which, when fully paid in, will without doubt put us out of debt. We had hoped that all bequests could go into an endowment fund. It ought so to be. But with outstanding bills it seems but right to discharge those obligations first.

A recent letter from Dr. Broomfield states that the $500 bequest from Fairmont, W. Va., cannot be paid in full because of the shrinkage of values in real estate; but that a check will be coming soon. Mr. J. A. Jordan, of Friendship on Shiloh charge, willed the Home $1,000, and the administrator thinks he can pay that about the first of the year.

Mr. and Mrs. A. S. Pickett, of Liberty, made wills to the Home. Out of Mr. Pickett's estate we have already gotten $2,750, and the administrator thinks we will get about $2,250 more. And out of Mrs. Pickett's estate he thinks we will get about $2,000. An effort is being made to settle up these·estates as early as possible, but those in charge are unable to tell us when final settlement will be made.

Thanksgiving is Just Ahead

The above bequests are going to put us out. of debt and put us a bit ahead, provided the supporters of the Home do not slacken their efforts and lessen their contributions. I was recently asked, "What will be the psychological effect of the Home's being out of debt?" I answered, "It ought to be good." But the falling off in contributions at the Anniversary Day indicated that at·least some of the people were depending upon those bequests to carry us. They will only carry us for a short·time. So we are laying our plans for the BEST-EVER Thanksgiving and Christmas offerings.

Our Thanksgiving letters have already gone out to pastors and Sunday school superintendents, urging a good offering. We trust that each of you will be boosters for a great Thanksgiving offering. And then if the offerings continue about as they have been for the last two years, we can go on at about the same rate. And if the offerings increase as times get better, we can do still better work.

Finances

In many ways we have had a good year, and the financial condition of the Home is improving. During the year we have had to put in a furnace in the boys' dormitory at a cost of $600. Special contributions took care of $262 of that, and the balance came out of the regular funds. A new laundry building was erected at a cost of $1,000. Special offerings for that amounted to $580.30, and the balance was paid out of regular funds. The old range in the girls' dormitory gave out completely and a new Majestic range has been put it at a cost of $309. This is not paid for, but the price goes into the sum total of our indebtedness. Then, too, the Anniversary offering this year lacked a little of being half what it was last year, and that counts out over $1,500. And an unfortunate wreck cost us all told $550.20.

We had hoped to have every cent of every outstanding obligation paid by this time, and that would have been done had our expectations in receipts been fulfilled. But taken all in all, we have had a wonderful year, the Lord has been good to us, and His people have responded well to the support of the orphan child. Our present indebtedness is about $3,500. The Thanksgiving offering should clear that up.

Looking to the Future

We have often expressed the desire, and we still have a longing desire, to see every debt of the Home cleared, and to see a central dining room and kitchen built, and some better arrangements made for the little children. We mean those under ten years of age.

This ought to be done looking toward Methodist union, so that we would have a bit better physical plant to carry into that union. Although there are two splendid children's homes in the state belonging to the M. E. Church, South, we feel that there will still be a need for this Home, and we should go into it with our physical plant in the best possible condition. Instead of waiting for the Methodist union, we should be up and doing so as to be happy about what we carry into it.

We are still carrying our boys to Sunday school and to church and to other places in a farm truck. On cold days and rainy days we have to make other shifts, so a new bus is almost a necessity. And, too, we are looking forward hopefully to the erection of a nice little building for a wood-working plant over by the laundry. It would be a wonderful help to our boys, and we confidently believe it would pay for itself within two or three years.

Financial Statement

The following figures for the year speak for themselves. And we are grateful to God and to His people for so good a showing. We have done our best, and we are thankful to Him for the privilege.

Financial Report

RECEIPTS

Duke endowment	$ 1,947.69
Churches, S. S., and C. E.	10,052.81
General Conference collection	282.00
Pickett Estate	2,750.00
Octagon coupons	589.96
Interest from endowment	221.10
Rebate on gas	71.48
Insurance Co., fire	72.50
Entertainments	7.42
Dividend from N. C. Bank	23.12
Homecoming day	1,509.49
Woman's Auxiliary	1,540.69
Farm	52.50
Relatives and friends	2,057.31
Total Receipts	$21,178.07
Received from Capt. A. M. Rankin	1,300.00
Total	$22,478.07

DISBURSEMENTS

All salaries	$ 4,267.25
Office supplies	222.76
Telephone and telegrams	134.59
Orphan Association	1.15
Insurance	357.04
Funeral wreaths	8.54
Finance and publicity	312.39
Service charges at bank	28.26
Food	3,722.97
Clothing	1,786.60
Car wreck	520.50
Laundry	368.82
Household supplies	809.50
Recreation	113.61
Travel care of children	2,063.41
Medicines	186.00
School supplies	521.53
Rent for land	76.75
Replacement and repairs, household	1,015.20

Repairs on the printing machine......................... 35.00
Extra institutional care.................................. 30.00
Farm supplies... 2,345.00
Repairs and replacement on farm........................ 901.70
Replacement of livestock................................ 40.00
Additional livestock 130.00
Laundry building.. 886.60
Paid money borrowed.................................... 150.00

Total disbursements...............................$21,988.61
Balance in Bank.. 489.46

Total $22,478.07

Respectfully submitted,

A. G. DIXON.

HONOR ROLL OF CHURCHES CONTRIBUTING TWELVE OR MORE TIMES DURING THE YEAR TO THE CHILDREN'S HOME

Alamance; Bethel, Center, Sapling Ridge and Rock Creek, Asheboro, Burlington, First Church and Fountain Place. Cleveland; Oak Grove, Lawndale and Kistlers-Union, Concord, Charlotte, Connellly Springs, Shady Grove, Creswell, Creswell. Danville. Denton, Canaan and Denton. Enfield, Enfield and Whitakers Chapel. Fallston, Friendship. Friendship Station. Forsythe; Maple Springs, Hickory Ridge, and Union Ridge. Gibsonville. Glen Raven, Haw River and Glen Raven. Graham. Granville, Rehoboth and Union Chapel. Grace Church. Calvary. Guilford; Fairfield, Mitchells Grove and Hickory Grove. Haw River, Friendship, Mizpah, Fair Grove, and Midway. Henderson. High Point; First Church, Lebannon and Welch Memorial. Kannapolis. Kernersville, Pine Grove. State Street, Bethesda and State Street. Lexington, First Church. Liberty. Mebane. Moriah. Mt. Hermon; Friendship, Bellemont and Mt. Hermon. Mt. Pleasant. Pleasant Union and Mt. Pleasant. North Davidson, Canaan and Mt. Pleasant. Orange, Efland and Union Grove. Pensacola. Pleasant Grove. Randleman; Mt. Lebanon, Level Cross and Worthville. Randolph, Shiloh and Bethany. Reidsville. Richland, Charlotte and Giles Chapel. Saxapahaw, Concord. Seagrove-Love Joy, Seagrove. Shiloh, Friendship and Shiloh. Spring Church; Lebannon, Pleasant Hill and Spring Church. Tabernacle, Julian and Tabernacle. Thomasville, Community Church and First Church. Vance, Harris Chapel and New Hope. Whitakers. West Forsythe, Baltimore and Pleasant Hill. Why Not, New Hope. Winston-Salem, First Church. Yarboroughs, Harmony and Yarboroughs chapel, Siler City, Vance, Gillburg.

The following facts are also worth thinking about. They are given here and may be published in the Journal or not, as you like.

Five other churches have contributed 10 times
Seven .... 9 times
Six .... 8 times
Six .... 7 times
Seven .... 6 times
Five .... 5 times
Seven .... 4 times

Thirteen .... 3 times
Nine .... 2 times
Seventeen .... 1 time.

And only twelve churches in the conference did not make any contribution to the Children's Home during this year. Lets make it unanimous during the coming year.

So far as a general response on the part of our people is concerned it has been the best year financially we have ever had. And this report shows conclusively that if each Church and Sunday school in the conference can be led to make a regular monthly offering to the Home there will always be funds to meet the actual needs. With expressions of gratitude to God and to His people for so good a year, this report is.

Respectfully submitted,

A. G. DIXON, Supt.

(H)   FINANCIAL STATEMENT OF CHILDREN'S HOME

Receipts

To. Ck's received from H. C. Staley, Treas. to
October 1, 1936 .... $1,733.33

Disbursements

By Ck. A. G. Dixon, Supt. (Maintenance) $1,300.00
By Ck. Atlantic & Piedmont Ins. Co. Ins. 406.20
By cash on Hand 27.13
————$1,733.33

Respectfully Submitted,

A. M. RANKIN, Treas.

(I)   REPORT OF COMMITTEE ON PARSONAGES

Your committee feels that the pastor and his family could render better service if the parsonages were more comfortable. We also realize that parsonage improvements usually originate with the pastor's family.

Therefore, we would encourage all pastors and their families to take an interest in improving their own parsonages and grounds, such as grassing the lawn, planting shrubbery, shade trees or fruit trees as needed. In this way pastors and their families will be a mutual blessing to each other. We also suggest that they take such an interest in the parsonage and grounds that it will encourage others to make their homes more attractive.

Your committee feels that the pastor's family should feel responsible for replacing unnecessary depreciations such as broken window panes and the like.

We recommend that a parsonage committee be elected by the Woman's Auxiliary or the Quarterly Conference of each charge. This committee to be composed of women of the church or charge who are successful in making their own homes comfortable and attractive and who are interested in the comfort and happiness of their pastor and family. This Committee should keep in touch with the pastor's wife to find out what is needed from time to time. After such needs are determined the Committee should see that they are provided as early as possible.

The Trustees should see that the parsonage is kept in good repair and painted.

Respectfully submitted,

E. A. BINGHAM, Chairman,
MRS. E. C. WALTERS,
Secretary.

(J) REPORT OF COMMITTEE ON ORDINANCES

The Christian Church has two ordinances, the Lord's Supper and Baptism.

We commend those who have had the Lord's Supper in charge at our Annual Conferences, for the way in which the services were conducted. Such services as these should be used as examples of similar services that can be held in each local church.

Definite preparations should be made for the observance of this ordinance. The pastor should prepare a sermon suitable for the occasion. Songs should be selected with great care.

The indifference on the part of many of these ordinances, especially that of the Lord's Supper, may be traced in many cases to the lack of proper instructions, hence we call upon our pastors to educate our people, especially the young, in the significance of these ordinances.

The effect of an impressive Lord's Supper is often lost by the lack of a suitable closing. We therefore urge that all other matters, such as announcements, etc., foreign to this service, be attended to as early in the service as possible.

Our denomination accepts Baptism by sprinkling, pouring, or immersion. We disapprove of rebaptism. This ordinance being commanded by the great Head of the Church, we therefore urge that it be not entered into lightly, but reverently, discreetly, and in the fear of God.

J. D. MORRIS,
D. T. HUSS,
J. LEO PITTARD,
RUSSELL CLINARD,
R. E. L. MOSER.

(K) REPORT OF THE PRESIDENT OF HIGH POINT COLLEGE

Brethren:

This formal report of the status of the college is my sixth to your annual conference session. I desire, at the outset, to express to you my appreciation for the kindly hearing you have given me on each occasion and the unfailing courtesy you have always extended me in your annual sessions.

The first part of the report will be somewhat routine, and yet necessary in order that you may have an appraisal of the general condition of the institution.

Enrollment

The thirteenth regular session began September 15, with approximately the same registration as the preceding fall; the peak for this year cannot be announced till after the second semester which begins next February. However, our number of boarding students is the largest since I have been president, one hundred and thirty-two. Twelve states, other than North Carolina, furnish twenty-four students.

Of this year's student body, 41.3% are Methodist Protestant; 28.2% are Methodist Episcopal; 13.7% are Baptist; 5.1% are Presbyterian; the remaining 13.1% is divided among 7 other church groups.

For the year ending September 1, the enrollment was highly gratifying; 311 in regular session, 75 in summer school (1935) and 160 in extension classes, making an all time record of 546. We anticipate this mark to be exceeded when the report is released for this year.

Finances

Again, we are glad to be able to report that current operations for the year ending September 1 showed no deficit. And I am wondering if the Conference comprehends just what it means when a college manages to keep its expenditures for current budget under its student income? I am sure you do not; only those whose experiences have or do relate them to actual operations can appreciate its full significance. It means a long hard pull at shaping and reshaping a budget, but we propose to maintain this record, if humanly possible, until the college debt is lifted.

Last conference I was able to announce that the churches of the Conference had met the challenge of the General Board of Education, and had raised from May, 1934, to May, 1935, from all sources, $5,768.23. And that amount exceeded by far any amount raised any one year since I had been president. Then another challenge was given the Conference, namely that the General Board would match dollar for dollar all monies raised in the Conference up to $4,000.00. I now report to you the answer to that challenge. From May, 1935, to May, 1936, the total raised was $3,419.83 from the following sources—churches of the Conference, $2,359.69; from the Branch, $837.39; bonds donated, $204.00; Loyalty League, $14.00; at college office, $4.75.

This total, as you can see, is $2,348.40 less than last year; accounted for in part by the difference in the amount from the Branch, and contribution through Loyalty League subscriptions. The churches directly, raised $655.14 less.

Debt Statement

Two years ago I called attention to the status of the obligations resting upon the Board of Education. I gave the figures at that time—1934, as compared with 1930, at the time the Bond Issue was created. My purpose in calling attention thus was to reassure the Conference and the church constituency against any apprehension as to increased debt as we were passing through the period of depression. That summary revealed that the debt was larger by about $22,000.00 after taking up the loss involved of $40,000.00 by the taking back from Saslow-Isacson of the Elm Street Property in Greensboro.

I am presenting today a chart showing totals of obligations of the Board of Education and the College (aside from current accounts); as of November, 1930, March, 1936, and November, 1936. This chart shows reductions as follows:

On Board of Education obligations, $85,407.53. Less than 6 years ago; and $101,305.09 less than 6 months ago. On College loans, $12,900.00 less than 6 years ago; and $5,685.00 less than 6 months ago.

The total indebtedness now of the Board for notes and bonds is $207,915.64; for college loans it is $12,600.00; and owing on the president's home is the amount of $8,450.00.

Our next move towards further liquidation of indebtedness is already under way. If the plan, agreed upon by the insurance company and myself, can be carried out this month, it will mean some further reduction of the debt, and the releasing of all endorsers from obligations at the Jefferson Standard; if this can be done, no individual will be endorsing anywhere for the college.

Following this, the bonds will be called in; and when we are able to call in the bonds, the whole issue will be cancelled and the Children's Home released from security status in connection with the college. While that security status is technical only, it is my very great desire to see the Home released.

Transfer of Property

At the Conference session of 1930, a resolution was adopted, signed by several members of the Conference, which stated, that insofar as this conference has the authority to so do—that the Board of Education and the Trustees of the College, are authorized and empowered to enter into any arrangement, by securing new charters, the dissolving of one corporation, the transfer of property or whatever may be necessary to create one central management of High Point College, in the interest of, and for the benefit of the Methodist Protestant Church.

We have kept in mind through these past years the intent of this resolution. In June, 1934, a new charter was obtained for the college. In 1935, the Board of Education by an unanimous vote moved to transfer the college property, the Elm Street property, and the President's Home to the College Trustees; and empowered me to arrange for such transfers. In September, the president's house was transferred; by unanimous vote of the Board of Education the Elm Street property was directed sold and the proceedings applied to debt reduction at the Jefferson Standard Life Insurance Company. (This of course obviates a transfer). The papers are ready to transfer the college land and buildings and equipment to the college trustees. All properties transferred are subject, of course, to the existing indebtedness thereon.

Present Expansion

We lived through the depression and we are coming out of that period with a forward look and a forward step.

FIRST: The Harrison Gymnasium, erected in 1933, but not completed is now being finished. Last year, dressing rooms in the wings for the students were completed with installation of showers, cement floors, lavatories, toilets, lights. A heating system was installed, and cement walk laid. This week we have laid cement floor in the basement; showers, toilets, sleeping quarters for visiting teams and an equipment room are all being put in. With this work done, we will have one of the most complete and usable gymnasiums of any small college in the state.

On October 6, work was renewed on the college athletic field, under W.P.A. supervision and through sponsorship of the City of High Point. The allocation of funds to complete the field calls for a total expenditure of about $30,000.00 for materials and labor. When completed we will have one of the finest stadiums in the state. Present plans, within the allocation, will give a concrete grandstand seating nearly 2500 persons; already there is a movement on in the city raise money to increase the seating capacity to about 7500 people.

Friday, October 30, the contract for the Wrenn Memorial Library was signed; Monday following the work started, and the contractor is driving ahead rapidly on the construction. The permit for general construction called for $24,000.00; the bids for electrical work, plumbing and heating will be received later; the completed building will probably cost nearly $30,000.00; the cut of the building is here and I hope you will all look at it. It will be a beautiful addition to the group on our campus, and meet a great need in our program, and be a fine witness to a generous spirit that would memorialize a great friend of the college.

Present Need

I shall try and sum them up briefly. *First*, that our pastors and people help us in the matter of student patronage. It is not too much to expect, is it, that our pastors seek to interest our own young people in and direct them to the college? The Conference, on several occasions, has pledged its members to seek new students for the institution—I am appealing that performance match the pledge. There ought not to be any difference on the part of our ministers to this phase of ministerial opportunity. Our Methodist Protestant Folks, with children ready for college ought not, with all good grace pass our own college by to send their sons and daughters elsewhere; some are doing this, many others are not. It seems to me that where such lack of interest of loyalty is evident our pastors might be of great service to the church. I am anxious to see 50% of our student body be Methodist Protestants, because of what it will mean later on to our church life in the state.

Second: Financial support by the Conference. The least the church in the state ought to want to do is to raise in full the $5,000.00 assessment each year. It ought to strive earnestly to do for the college what the General Board will do annually for us. And this year, especially it must be done, to meet our needs. The equipment for the Library, certain materials which we must furnish for the athletic field, and interest make our requirements about $18,000.00. If this conference will place itself squarely on record saying it will pledge itself to see that its $5,000.00 is raised by May, 1937—I can promise, that from certain *sure* sources, I will have the remaining $13,000.00 before next Commencement.

I want the Conference to see what the college, this year, is giving to children from Methodist Protestant homes; in scholarships, $2700; in self-help positions, $4500; a total of $7200—112% more than the Conference gave the college from May, 1935, to May, 1936. Certainly in dollars and cents, the Conference ought to give the college more than the college gives the Conference!

Tomorrow

To me the vision is quite clear—a bigger and better institution! This is true, whether it be a Methodist Protestant College or a Methodist College. Confidently, I hope to see it by 1940 a Methodist College. But either way—bigger and better.

I vividly recall my first presence, as president of the college, at your annual session. It was in this church in 1930. I can feel again the atmosphere of that session. Some of you will recall that my first speech before this body was a plea for time and opportunity for High Point College; I asked for your faith in the future, your patience with the program, your cooperation in constructive effort, and your pledge to its purpose; after six years I come to you today and simply state that I am confident an unbiased verdict will say that the record vindicated what was my confidence and my hope— and that we will agree progress has been made such as justifies our hope for tomorrow.

I appeal, therefore, to the whole Conference to go with me the whole way—in your prayers, in your patronage, in your support; in spirit and in attitude as individuals; in a whole hearted cooperation as a church group. How the church stands by is being watched by the state, by the community, by Methodism, by 400 graduates and by 300 students. STAND BY, STAND BY—and ultimately we shall see the travail of our souls and be satisfied.

Recommendations

FIRST: That the Conference appoint P E. Lindley, P. S. Kennett, and N. M. Harrison for work with the college.

SECOND: That the Conference pledge itself to an unceasing effort to raise the $5,000.00 college assessment by May 1, 1936; and that the months of March and April be designated College Months.

THIRD: That our ministers undertake to seek out and direct those young people of our churches, who are prospective college students for next year, towards enrollment at High Point next September; and cooperate thus with the president of the college in securing a 50% Methodist Protestant student body.

FOURTH: That the following resolution be adopted: "Whereas, by the will of the late A. S. Pickett of Liberty, N. C., certain provisions therein made bequests to High Point College; and

Whereas, settlement of the estate will eventually bring to the College monies totalling about $6,000.00; therefore, be it Resolved, that the Conference hereby record its gratitude that Dr. Pickett so remembered the college, and voices its appreciation that it is being made available at a time to meet needs in the growth and development of the college.

Fraternally,

GIDEON I. HUMPHREYS, President.

(L) REPORT OF THE COMMITTEE ON CHURCH MUSIC

Since music is probably the most universal language, and is the means by which more people are led into a worship experience than any other, we should realize the importance of using the best type of music in our church services. The Committee realizes that the need for better church music has been presented to this Annual Conference many times and each time some suggestions are offered to encourage a better class of music in our churches. We do not, therefore, propose to suggest anything new but merely to remind you of many things that have been offered before.

We see evidences of progress in many of our churches. We commend those pastors and people of the churches where cheap music and jazz are being replaced by a higher type of music. We are thankful that more of our people are learning to appreciate better music. We commend those churches that have refused to buy cheap song books, which are equally cheap in quality as well as price, and have furnished their church with creditable hymn books.

We also commend the North Carolina Council of Religious Education for the place it has given in its program to the development and encouraging of better church music. We thank Rev. E. Lester Ballard for the large part he has played in encouraging better music in our churches.

While progress is being made, we realize that there is yet much room for improvement in most of our churches. There are a few churches where cheap song books are in use and a low grade of music is used. We recommend therefore,

1. The use of the New Methodist Hymnal in all of the churches where practicable. If cheaper books are to be bought, seek the advice of some capable music teacher or director.

2. That churches buy enough hymn books that each worshiper may have access to one.

3. That a young people's choir be organized in each church, where practicable.

4. That the North Carolina Conference Council of Religious Education continue its efforts to promote better music.

5. That public school music teachers be used as much as possible to help promote better church music.

6. That pastors carefully select hymns to be used in every worship service before the hour of service, consulting, if necessary with the director of music and the pianist of the church.

7. That churches promoting singing schools insist upon the use of their own hymn books rather than those recommended for sale by the singing masters.

8. That regular periods for learning new hymns be established in each church, the time and place to be determined by the local church.

9. Realizing the power and inspiration in congregational singing, we urge that more emphasis be placed upon congregational hymn singing.

The Committee,

J. W. BRAXTON,
D. R. CONNELL.

(M) REPORT OF THE COMMITTEE ON MISSIONS ·

The philosophy of Christian Missions is fundamental to the life of the church. The Christian church grew out of missionary propaganda. Christian Missions is not only "good news" but a principal of sustaining life to those who tell the "good news." Missions is not an added enterprise assumed by the church, but a principal that is inherent and co-existent with the very nature of the Gospel itself. It is a part of God's redemptive plan not only for the heathen, but for the paganism still remaining in our hearts and churches.

Christian Missions furnish a medium for the cultivation of the good seed of the Kingdom seeking expression in my life. The "good news" of Christ's salvation to be good news to me must be told by me. Using the church as a figure: The altars of the church represents where my heart was "strangely warmed," the windows of the church represent God's love and mercy shining in on my soul, and the doors of the church represent the "other ward" leading of the new found joy, or Christian Missions. The doors of the church are as indispensable as the windows and the altar. Christian Missions gives direction—heads us off to do something about it.

We are hearty in our support of the work of the Board of Missions at home and abroad. We exhort our people to come to the rescue of these worthy enterprises with their dollars, that in turn God may enrich our lives and pour out his blessings upon us.

We deplore that our people are not better informed as to the benevolent enterprises. We urge that our pastors earnestly endeavor to get to our people missionary information, such as our *Missionary Record,* including our *Methodist Protestant Herald* and *Methodist Protestant-Recorder,* and all other missionary materials which are available. Without missionary information there can be no real interest.

Recommendations

We recommend that Rev. J. F. Minnis, a minister in this conference, be loaned to the Board of Missions to go as a missionary to India.

We recommend, as an aid to larger offerings for missions on Special Days, the sending of envelopes, supplied by the Board, direct to the people, either by special agencies or through the mail. We believe that any expenses entailed will be fully repaid by increased offerings.

We recommend, as an aid to putting on Special Day programs for missions, the appointment of committee at the beginning of the conference year, whose responsibility will be the preparation of these programs. And in this connection, we recommend that pastors send the name of the chairmen of these committees to the Secretary of the Board of Missions that material may be sent direct to the committee.

Respectfully submitted,

J. CLYDE AUMAN, Chairman,
MRS. J. M. BAITY, Secretary.

(N) REPORT OF TRUSTEES OF DISTRICT PARSONAGE

Receipts

1935
11– 1 Balance on hand ....$ 57.55
12–24 J. H. Allen, Treasurer 268.57
Rents 511.50
————$ 837.62

Disbursements

12–16 Plastering 126 Tate Street ....$ 14.00
12–21 Repairs 909 W. College Place 3.75
12–24 J. Norman Wills, Treasurer, Interest....... 24.00
12–28 Mrs. H. A. Garrett—Interest 100.00
12–30 Cody Realty Company—Interest 150.00
1936
3– 5 L. W. Flythe Ins. Co. 909 W. College......... 22.50
3–10 F. H. Craft Insurance—126 Tate Street.... 15.00
3–31 F. R. Hutton Ins. Co.—126 Tate Street...... 15.00
3–31 Cody Realty Company—Interest.............. 30.00
4–10 Repairs chimney—126 Tate Street............ 11.00
4–30 Cody Realty Company—Interest............. 35.00
5–29 Cody Realty Company—Interest............. 35.00
7–27 Cody Realty Company—Interest............. 50.00
7–27 Odell Hardware Co., on account.............. 12.32
8–28 Cody Realty Company—Interest............. 6.17
10– 2 Mrs. H. A. Garrett—Interest............. 20.00
10– 2 Odell Hardware Company—on account....... 15.00
10– 2 Wiring—126 Tate Street 6.00
10– 6 Mitchell-Clark Company—126 Tate Street.. 8.04
11– 2 J. Norman Wills, Treasurer—Interest....... 24.00
11– 2 Mrs. H. A. Garrett—Interest.............. 50.00
11– 2 Home Building Material Co.—on account.... 25.00
11– 2 City of High Point—Paving Assn............. 94.83
11– 2 Cash balance 71.01
————$ 837.62

Liabilities

D. A. McLaurin—Note ....$ 150.00
Mrs. H. A. Garrett—Mortgage.............. 5,750.00
Mrs. H. A. Garrett—Interest........$1,897.50
Less payments 170.00
———— 1,727.50
Metropolitan Life Ins. Co.—Mortgage........ 3,500.00
Metropolitan Life Ins. Co.
—Interest Nov. 1, 1936.... 105.00
Superannuate Fund Society 800.00
Superannuate Fund Society—Interest........ 194.00
Odell Hardware Co. 26.55
Paving Assessment 207.78
W. D. Waynick—Repairs 126 Tate Street.. 290.38
Total ....————$12,751.21

Respectfully submitted,

F. R. STOUT, Treasurer.

FUND SOCIETY

Receipts

1935				
Nov.	1.	Balance on hand	$	59.94
Nov.	10.	Offering Memorial Service		35.00
	15.	Board Church Extension, Interest		30.00
	29.	J. H. Allen, Treasurer		1,454.78
Dec.	27.	Trustees President's Parsonage, Int.		24.00
1936				
Mch.	25.	Interest collected		27.00
Apr.	14.	Interest collected		33.00
July	30.	Dividend N. C. Bank & Trust Co. (In liquidation)		9.26
Aug.	13.	Dividend N. C. Bank & Trust Co. (In liquidation)		6.79
Sept.	14.	Interest collected		33.00
	21.	Loan repaid		900.00
	21.	Interest on Loan collected		27.00
Nov.	4.	Trustees President's Parsonage, Int.		24.00
	1.	Rents Guilford Avenue House, net		378.52
				$3,042.29

Disbursements

1935				
Nov.	16.	Probating and registering Deed	$	1.50
	29.	Mrs. C. L. Whitaker		10.00
		Mrs. W. C. Lassiter		10.00
		Mrs. J. B. O'Briant		10.00
		Mrs. N. Brittain		10.00
		Mrs. C. A. Cecil		65.00
		Mrs. L. W. Gerringer		65.00
		Mrs. J. F. Dosier		50.00
		Mrs. W. C. Kennett		40.00
		Mrs. C. W. Saunders		25.00
		Mrs. J. W. Hulin		25.00
		Mrs. C. J. Edwards		25.00
		Mrs. W. P. Martin		10.00
		Mrs. C. H. Whitaker		50.00
		Mrs. E. G. Lowdermilk		50.00
		Rev. G. W. Holmes		110.00
		Rev. T. F. McCulloch		110.00
		Rev. W. M. Pike		110.00
		Rev. W. F. Ashburn		110.00
		Rev. W. T. Totten		110.00
		Rev. H. S. B. Thompson		110.00
		Rev. A. L. Hunter		110.00
		Rev. W. F. Kennett		120.00
		Rev. G. F. Millaway		120.00
		Rev. H. L. Powell		110.00
Dec.	27.	Odell Hardware Co., Bal. on Roofing, G. Ave.		100.79
1936				
Sept.	21.	Funds loaned, secured by Mortgage		500.00
	30.	Funds loaned, secured by Mortgage		400.00
	26.	City Greensboro, Bal. Paving Guil. Ave.		77.92
		Cash for Postage		3.00

Oct. 19. Odell Hardware Co., Roofing Pearson St.   119.62
                                                    ————$2,767.83

Nov. 5. Balance in Security National Bank......... $ 274.46

J. NORMAN WILLS, Treasurer.

Examined and found correct.

J. A. BURGESS,
EDW. SUITS,
Auditing Committee.

(P) REPORT OF THE BOARD OF MANAGERS OF THE SUPERANNUATED FUND SOCIETY

We have elected, and submit for your approval, the following members of the Board of Managers: To take the place of **F. R. Harris**, deceased, L. L. Wren; to take the place of J. B. Ogburn, deceased, W. T. Hanner. As an additional member, to make the number provided by the charter (nine) T. J. Whitehead.

The other six members of the Board of T. M. Johnson, J. A. Burgess, S. R. Harris, J. D. Williams, Edward Suits, and J. Norman Wills. We request that the names of the members of the Board of Managers be inserted in the Journal, with those of other Conference Boards and committees.

J. NORMAN WILLS, Secretary.

We recommend the following appropriations, to be paid by the Treasurer from funds now and in hand, and to be received from the Conference Treasurer.

Mrs. C. L. Whitaker ....$	20.00
Mrs. W. C. Lassiter	20.00
Mrs. J. B. O'Briant	20.00
Mrs. N. Brittain	20.00
Mrs. W. P. Martin	20.00
Mrs. W. F. Kennett	20.00
Mrs. C. W. Saunders	30.00
Mrs. J. W. Hulin	30.00
Mrs. C. J. Edwards	30.00
Mrs. W. C. Kennett	50.00
Mrs. C. H. Whitaker	60.00
Mrs. E. G. Lowdermilk	60.00
Mrs. J. F. Dosier	65.00
Mrs. C. A. Cecil	75.00
Mrs. L. W. Gerringer	90.00
Rev. G. W. Holmes	130.00
Rev. T. F. McCulloch	130.00
Rev. W. M. Pike	130.00
Rev. W. F. Ashburn	130.00
Rev. W. T. Totten	130.00
Rev. H. S. B. Thompson	130.00
Rev. A. L. Hunter	130.00
Rev. H. L. Powell	130.00
Rev. T. A. Williams	130.00

$2,080.00

Respectfully submitted,

J. NORMAN WILLS, Secretary.

(Q)   REPORT OF THE TREASURER OF THE ROBERTS BEQUEST

Receipts

1935
Nov. 4.   Balance on hand (see minutes, page 60)..$ 213.73
1936
April 6.   Interest collected..   63.00
May 2.   Interest collected..   120.00
July 30.   Dividend N. C. Bank & Trust Co. in
              liquidation) 144.24
Oct. 15.   Interest collected ....
Nov. 4.   Interest collected ....

Disbursements

Loans to Students
         Lee Moser ....$ 120.00
         Joseph F. Coble 125.00
         Forrest Wagoner 75.00
         W. M. Howard 50.00
         J. Leo Pittard 50.00
For postage 1.00

                                                    $ 421.00

Balance in Security National Bank .... $ 302.97
Due by North Carolina Bank & Trust Co. (in
    liquidation) .... $ 317.33
Students Loans to date, net $12,912.87
    Investments are the same as last year.   See minutes, page 60.

J. NORMAN WILLS, Treasurer.

(R)   REPORT OF THE TREASURER OF THE FULLER BEQUEST

1935
Nov. 1.—Balance in Guilford National Bank, Saving Dept. ....$ 18.32
1936
May. 6.   Dividend United Bank & Trust Co. (in liquidation).. 44.62

Nov. 1.   Balance in Guilford National Bank................................$ 62.94
         Balance due by United Bank & Trust Co. $116.00
         Stock in United Bank Building Co. 42.00
         One Note for Student Loan..$200.00

J. NORMAN WILLS, Treasurer.

(S) REPORT ON BOUNDARY COMMITTEE

The Boundary Committee beg leave to make the following recommendations:

1. That Fairfield be detached from Lincoln charge and same be made a station.

2. That Love's Grove be detached from Midland Charge and attached to Friendship, and that Pine Bluff be detached from Midland and same be made a station. That Mill Grove be made a station and that the name Midland be dropped from the plan of appointments.

3. That Flint Hill and Macedonia be detached from Seagove-Love Joy charge and attached to Why Not.

4. That Pine Grove be detached from Why Not charge and attached to Mt. Zion charge.

N. G. BETHEA, Secretary.

(T) REPORT OF BOARD OF CHURCH EXTENSION

To the North Carolina Annual Conference,
Methodist Protestant Church,
Albemarle Sessions, November 4-9, 1936.

We, your Board of Church Extension, beg to submit the following as the record of receipts and disbursements during the Conference year:

Receipts

Nov. 6, 1935	Bal in First Nat. Bank (Asheboro, N. C.)......	14.31
Nov. 14, 1935	Ck from J. H. Allen, Treasurer ....$	500.00
Dec. 7, 1935	Ck from J. H. Allen, Treasurer	567.01
May 15, 1936	Ck from Miss Sallie R. Taylor For note issued May 14, 1936..................	1,000.00

$2,081.32

Disbursements

1935

Nov. 14.	Check R. L. Vickery (Appropriation)	50.00
Nov. 14.	Check Mrs. Geo. L. Curry (Interest) ....$	69.00
Nov. 14.	Check J. Norman Wills, Treasurer, Superannuated Fund Society (Interest)..	30.00
Nov. 14.	Check Mrs. Mary Hopkins, (Interest)......	30.00
Nov. 14.	Check J. L. Brinkley (Interest)...............	30.00
Nov. 14.	Check D. R. Connell (Interest).................	30.00

1935

Dec. 3.	Check J. L. Love (Appropriation)............	25.00
Dec. 3.	Check Lee Moser (Appropriation).............	50.00
Dec. 3.	Check L. S. Helms (Appropriations)........	100.00
Dec. 7.	Check Weaverville Ch. (Appropriation)....	75.00
Dec. 7.	Check Rankin Mem. Ch. (Appropriation)	100.00
Dec. 7.	Check J. L. Brinkley (Back Interest)........	100.00
Dec. 7.	Check J. W. Walser (Part note & Interest)	128.00
Dec. 7.	Check J. E. Pritchard (Interest)..............	48.00
Dec. 7.	Check E. Lee Chambliss, Admr. M. P. Chamblis Balance due on appropriation....	50.00

| Dec. 24. | Check J. L. Love (Add. appropriation).... | 25.00 |
| Dec. 24. | Check Tax on checks accrued in 1934 at bank | .12 |

1936
Jan. 3.	Check Miss Mary McCulloch (Interest)..	60.00
May 15.	Check Mrs. Mary Hopkins (Note & Int.)	514.33
May 15.	Check J. W. Walser (Bal. note & Int.)....	407.60
May 15.	Check J. L. Brinkley (Bal. on back Int.)..	100.00
Oct. 16.	Check D. R. Connell (Interest)	30.00
Nov. 6.	Balance in First National Bank Asheboro, N. C.	28.52

$2,081.32

We attach list of outstanding notes now owing by the Board which is all the indebtedness except current interest which approximates about $300.00

Respectfully submitted,

J. E. PRITCHARD, Chairman
W. L. WARD, Secy. & Treas.

List of outstanding notes of the Board of Church Extension of the North Carolina Annual Conference of November 6, 1936.

J. L. Brinkley	$ 500.00
Mrs. Geo. L. Curry	575.00
D. R. Connell	500.00
Superannuated Fund Society	500.00
J. E. Pritchard	800.00
Mrs. Geo. R. Brown	325.00
Miss Mary Wills McCulloch	1,000.00
Miss Sally B. Taylor	1,000.00

$5,200.00

J. E. PRITCHARD,
                Chairman
W. L. WARD,
        Secretary & Treasurer.

(U)   REPORT OF EDITOR OF THE METHODIST PROTESTANT HERALD

Receipts
Balance carried over from last year	$ 426.59
Received on subscriptions	3,381.56
Received on subsidy from churches	424.63
Received on subsidy from Boards and Institutions....	487.00
Received from advertising	14.00

Total receipts from all sources $4,733.78

Disbursements
To McCulloch and Swain, printing Herald	$3,680.26
To bookkeeping	212.00
To mailing Herald	106.73

To editorial expense 1934-35 .... 101.36
To editorial expense, 1935-36 .... 101.15
To stamps, postal cards, envelopes, Miscellaneous
    printing 55.30

    Total disbursements $4,256.80
Cash in Bank ....$ 476.98

    Total $4,733.78

J. E. PRITCHARD.

Examined and found correct.

J. NORMAN WILLS,
J. ELWOOD CARROLL,
Audit Committee.

REPORT OF AUDIT COMMITTEE

We, your committee to audit the books of the Editor of the Methodist Protestant Herald, find the books are beautifully and accurately kept. We commend the Editor, Dr. J. E. Pritchard, and the Book Keeper, Miss Mary C. McCulloch, for their excellent service.

J. NORMAN WILLS
J. ELWOOD CARROLL.

Nov. 13, 1936.

(V) REPORT OF COMMITTEE ON METHODIST PROTESTANT HERALD

The Methodist Protestant Herald has had a very successful year, for which we are grateful. It is very gratifying that more of our people are reading and appreciating the paper. We consider the Herald an essential agency in the promotion of the interests of our Conference and the institutions of our Church.

We are profoundly grateful to Dr. J. E. Pritchard for his splendid work during the past year, and the very efficient manner in which he has managed the paper.

We also express our profound gratitude to the members of Calvary Church for their splendid spirit of co-operation in permitting their pastor to give of his time to the work of the Herald.

We heartily commend those charges which have raised their apportionment for the McCulloch Memorial Fund, the Herald Subsidy and subscription quotas. The pastors and Herald agents on the various charges deserve much praise for their efforts to increase the circulation of the paper.

The Committee makes the following recommendations:

1. That the President of the Annual Conference, Dr. R. M. Andrews, be the Editor and Business Manager of the Herald for the ensuing year.

2. That out of the cash balance now on hand the retiring Editor be given $100 for editorial expenses of the past year.

3. That the subsidy be apportioned to the various organizations as follows: Woman's Work, $100.00; Children's Home, $100.00; Council of Religious Education, $50.00; Annual Conference, $200.00; and that the basis of apportionment on the charges be the same as last year.

4. That a Herald Subscription Committee, composed of Dr. C. W. Bates, Dr. N. G. Bethea and F. R. Stout, be elected.

5. That pastors appoint Herald agents to work with him in securing subscriptions. Emphasis from the pulpit is not enough; personal solicitation is also necessary.

6. That the Chairman of the various districts endeavor to promote the interest of the Herald by giving it a proper place on the programs of their district meetings.

T. G. MADISON, Chairman,
C. B. WAY, Secretary.

(W)   REPORT OF CONFERENCE TRUSTEES

Receipts

1935				
Nov.	1.	Balance on hand (see minutes, page 59)	$ 76.42	
1936				
Nov.	1.	Rents Rocky Mount House, less Repairs and Agent's Commission	129.01	
Nov.	1.	Rent Johnson Cottage, less Repairs and Commission	64.00	
Nov.	1.	Rent Pearson St. House, less Repairs and Commission	212.76	
		Dividend from N. C. Bank & Trust Co. (In liquidation)	2.89	
			$	485.08

Disbursements

1935				
Dec.	2.	On Loan Pearson Street Property........$	60.00	
		Interest	38.40	
1936				
Feb.	14.	City of Greensboro, Benefit Assessment..	7.27	
April	10.	Repairs, Pearson Street	37.75	
	16.	Repairs Pearson Street	64.00	
	16.	Repairs Pearson Street Garage	28.78	
June	1.	On Loan, Pearson Street	60.00	
		Interest	36.60	
Aug.	6.	Insurance, Rocky Mount	8.50	
Oct.	5.	On Assessment, City of Greensboro, Paving and Storm Sewer, Ross Avenue (Johnson Cottage)	16.19	
		Interest on the same	5.83	
	16.	Labor, putting on New Roof, Pearson St.	52.50	
			$	415.82
		Balance in Security National Bank........$		69.26
		Amount due us by N. C. Bank & Trust Co. (in liquidation)		6.36

Amount owing on loan for Repairs to
Pearson Street House ....$ 1,160.00
Amount owing City of Greensboro, Pav-
ing etc. 137.54

On April 2 a severe tornado struck our city, and the Pearson Street house sustained considerable damage.. The repairs which seemed necessary were made, but it later developd that a new roof must be put on. This property was bequeathed to the Conference by the late Milton Coble and wife, for the benefit of superannuates. In re-roofing the house, it was found necessary to pay for the materials direct from Superannuate funds, which, will, however, be repaid as further rents are collected.

J. NORMAN WILLS, Treasurer.

Examined and found correct.

J. R. HUTTON,
L. L. WREN
Auditing Committee.

(X) REPORT OF THE FACULTY

That a vote of appreciation be extended to N. G. Bethea, retiring secretary of the Conference Faculty, for seventeen years of service.

William Miller Howard, Jr., having completed the Seminary course, and having fulfilled the requirements of the Discipline, is recommended for ordination as an Elder.

On motion this resolution was offered for your approval:-

1. Resolved that each person applying for admission to the North Carolina Annual Conference of the Methodist Protestant Church be required to furnish the following information:-

(1) Date and place of birth, Names of father and mother.
(2) When converted, time of joining the church, and the charge.
(3) Give educational qualifications. Give names of schools attended.
(4) When licensed to preach and what Quarterly Conference issued the license? How long you have preached and what charges served? .

2. That the above facts be enrolled in the records of this Faculty, and published in the Conference minutes when ordained.

F. S. Wagoner, J. F. Coble, E. P. Hamilton, W. J. Neese, J. Leo Pittard, F. A. Wright, O. L. Easter, R. L. Moser, C. P. Morris, Aubert M. Smith, G. B. Ferree and W. C. Clark be recommended to the Stationing Committee for work if needed.

The Faculty recommends that no one shall be admitted to the Conference course of study until he shall have finished at least two years of study in an A Grade College.

However, those who do not meet the above requirement may be used by the President of the Annual Conference in his discretion as supply pastors.

No one, though he has finished two, or even four years in an A Grade College, shall be employed by the Conference for more than two years without taking the Seminary or Conference Course.

Any preacher may be ordained when he has complied with the Law of the Church as given on page 62 of the 1936 Discipline.

W. C. Clark has passed "Principles of Preaching," "Parlimentary Law," "Sermon on Repentance," "Objectives in Religious Education," "Personal Salvation," and "Robert's Rules of Order."

We recommend that R. E. L. Moser, Herman Yokeley, F. A. Wright and E. P. Hamilton be enrolled in the first year of the Conference Course.

S. W. TAYLOR, Chairman,
H. FREO SURRATT, Secretary.

(Y)   REPORT OF THE COMMITTEE ON EVANGELISM

Evangelism takes us to the very heart and center of the Church's program. To evangelize the world is the supreme task of the Church. Such a task is God given. Christ, the great Head of the Church, charged the Church with this responsibility. The Church dare not trifle with nor be indifferent to this responsibility. The Church dare not side-track this her primary obligation for other causes. The Church dare not so give herself to any program, however noble and worthy, if in so doing she neglects her high privilege, yea, her God-given task of ministering to the soul that wanders and strays from God's fold and the Christian way of life.

Your Committee on Evangelism believes that the program of Christian evangelism includes the following items: *First*—winning souls for Christ. There are many methods which may be used in doing this.

a. The revival meeting. We believe in the revival meeting. We believe that the best place for a person to accept Christ is at the altar of the Church. A revival meeting should be held in every church at least once during the conference year and if possible no time limit should be set as to the duration of such meeting. Careful planning, much prayer by individuals and groups, the securing of a list of the names of those unsaved and back-slidden, should all be done prior to the beginning of the revival services. A revival meeting should never be conducted merely through custom, but because the souls of sinful men need to be saved and the church brought to a deeper consecration of life.

b. Personal touch. Many unsaved people never attend a revival meeting. They ought to, but they do not. The altar is the best place for them to surrender their lives to Christ. But if they will not come to the altar, shall we allow them to die in their sins? Certainly not. Christ's saving and redeeming power is not limited to time and place. Whenever and wherever a life meets His conditions of discipleship that life becomes a new creature in Christ Jesus. Then let us go into the homes, places of business, anywhere in order that we may win a soul for Christ. When they have accepted Christ they will gladly come to the altar of the Church and dedicate their lives to Him and His program.

c. Pastor's instruction class. The pastor may gather about him a group for the specific purpose of instructing them in the

Christian way of life. He must not teach them as though they were already Christians, but teach them how to get hold of God, how to know Christ as their own personal Saviour and what it means to consecrate their lives to Him and His cause.

d. A two-month period of evangelistic preaching supplemented by personal work and pastor's instruction class. During this period the pastor's sermons are evangelistic in their appeal. He and his people do personal work. A class of instruction and training in the Christion way of life is conducted and every possible thing done to reach the lost.

e. Special occasions and days. Easter and the anniversary of Pentecost lend themselves easily to an evangelistic appeal. Many of our churches are already using these occasions in this way; all of them should whenever it is at all possible. While we should regularly observe all denominational Special Days and diligently seek for the largest possible offering for our various Denominational Boards, let the major emphasis be always on the consecration of life to Christ and His Church. We urge our churches to cooperate with the National Preaching Mission in so far as they possibly can.

f. That the pastors get in touch with Rev. W. A. Melvin, Secretary of Evangelism, Baltimore, Md., for helps for personal evangelism.

Second—the Christian nurture and development of the life which has been won for Christ. The new Christian needs the love, counsel, admonition, prayers and interest of the church membership. When a new member is received the church members promise to do these things; but, alas, too often the promise is neglected and the new Christian stumbles and falls. One of the great sins which can be laid at the door of the Church is just this. Not one of us would neglect a new-born babe. The child's needs make us alert and diligently, lovingly we endeavor to satisfy those needs. The child's cry reaches the depths of our hearts and we do our best to relieve and comfort. But, alas, the needs of the new Christian do not stir our complacent lives, find no place in our prayers and, though we may hear their cries of wretchedness and suffering as they are caught again in the old sinful habits, too often we only criticize and condemn instead of lifting them up by love and prayer where they may again get hold of God and have restored unto them the joys of Christ's salvation.

Third—the life which has been won for Christ and is being nurtured in the Christian way of life definitely enlisted in Christ's service. Christianity is a religion of activity and service. No folded hands, for religion is not an easy chair, but a cross. The church member who loses his interest in Christ's program soon loses his faith in God and becomes cold, indifferent and backslidden in heart. Inactivity kills faith. Inactivity, though forced upon him, paralized the faith of John the Baptist, the once brave, courageous herald of the Christ. It has lost none of its power. Every church member ought to be enlisted in some phase of kingdom service.

This is your Committee's conception of the program of Christian Evangelism. We urge our pastors and people to give this program first place in our hearts, in our prayers and in our churches. If we fail, in other matters, let us never fail here. If we neglect other things, let us never lose the holy passion of seeking the lost. As Jesus came to seek and save the lost, may we diligently, prayerfully, faithfully seek the lost and bring them to Christ in order that they may be saved through HIM.

F. W. PASCHALL,
G. H. HENDRY,
C. G. ISLEY,
R. A. HUNTER,
J. L. TROLLINGER.

(Z)   COMMISSION ON METHODIST COOPERATION

The Annual Meeting of the Commission on Methodist Cooperation was held in the office of the Editor of the North Carolina *Christian Advocate*, Greensboro, on Friday, October 2, 1936. Representatives were present from the three Methodist bodies. As a result of our deliberations the following message is presented for your consideration:

Since our last report the General Conferences of the Methodist Episcopal and the Methodist Protestant Churches have adopted by overwhelming votes the Plan of Union proposed by the Commissions on Union of the three Methodisms. It is now being acted upon by the Annual Conferences of the two bodies whose General Conferences have passed it down to them. None of the Annual Conferences of the Methodist Episcopal Church has opposed the adoption of the Plan of Union. On the contrary the vote in every case has been almost unanimous. As the Commission meets twelve Annual Conferences of the Methodist Protestant Church have voted upon the Plan of Union. Nine have voted for it, three against it. But it is unquestioned that more than the necessary two-thirds of the Annual Conferences will approve it in their sessions during October and November. The General Conference of the Methodist Episcopal Church, South, not having met to pass upon it, action is of course deferred; but the sentiment and attitude toward union as unofficially expressed is so unmistakably favorable that it is only a matter of the necessary lapse of time until the Plan of Union will have been adopted by the three branches of Methodism involved, and we shall go on to the holding of the Uniting Conference. But this can apparently not be held before 1939.

"The King's business requireth haste," but not too much haste. We would caution our folks in each of the Annual Conferences and in all the local churches not to be precipitate; but to prepare themselves for the ultimate union of our forces. This can best be done with each group carrying on its own work; developing and utilizing its own resources spiritual and physical; but at the same time encouraging and taking advantage of every possible opportunity for friendly contacts and cooperation. To this end we would suggest:

1. The holding of evening services together wherever practical, alterating, if possible, between church houses, the pastors taking turns in preaching; or making any other arrangements as to services as shall emphasize this sense of unity.

2. That wherever possible the ministers of the three groups assist each other in the holding of revival services. The Commission might assist in securing pastors for this exchange of evangelistic effort.

3. That the pastors of the three Methodisms take advantage of the Pastors' Summer Schools conducted by each group, attending

the one nearest them, and thereby becoming better acquainted with the personnel in the several conferences. An invitation is extended by the Duke School of Religion and the officers of the Pastors' Conference of the Methodist Episcopal Church, South, for the ministers of the other two Methodisms to attend and share in its benefits. The acceptance of the invitation is, of course, at the pleasure of each group. But the Commission commends it to the brethren as one means of attaining this sense of approaching oneness.

4. That we suggest again to the officers of the Annual Conference Councils of Religious Education, or similar bodies, the advantage of holding group meetings in which the three Methodisms shall be represented wherever possible, for the training of Christian workers, whether in Conference assemblies or in local church groups. If this does not seem advisable at this stage, then we would suggest that wherever one group is holding such schools or assemblies the others be invited to attend and participate.

5. That we undertake again the holding of joint gatherings for mutual fellowship where the principles and programs, the historic background, the common heritage and task of Methodism, may be emphasized.

The Commission on Methodist Cooperation created by the three branches of the Methodist Church in North Carolina is probably unique. To our knowledge nothing like it exists anywhere in America. It may well be that through its work the approach to union will be much more easily effected here than elsewhere. The success of the union movement will depend much on that approach.

The Commission, therefore, asks the hearty support of each conference, pastor and local church, to the end that its work, when and if union is consummated, may be the more effective in bringing about a real union of our forces in North Carolina; and set an example for the Conferences and churches of the uniting Methodisms in the other States.

M. T. PLYLER, Chairman,
C. W. BATES, Secretary.

(AA)   PASTORAL WORK

Many workers are called by God into his spiritual harvest fields, and he endows them with gifts and graces according to the fields in which he designs that they shall work. To none does he give greater and more varied gifts than to those whom he calls to be the pastors of his people. Their work is as varied as life itself, and as constant as the rising and setting of the sun. The pastor's program of service comprehends life in all of its phases. In point of time the range is from the cradle to the grave. In point of kind the range three fold—the mind, the soul and the body. The pastor must be food and raiment and shelter to the needy; he must be wisdom to the unenlightened; light to the blind; strength to the weak; courage to the faltering; solace to the sorrowing; and a beacon light to those who walk in paths of danger and death. He is the shepherd, and every need of the flock must be his need, and every opportunity of the flock must be his opportunity. In a very real and special sense the pastor is God's man to those whom he is sent to serve.

He must, therefore, be a comfort and guide to them in the daily affairs of life. But more: he must be God's messenger to them in the preaching of his word. His ministry as priest must be to his people the molifying ointment that will heal the brokenhearted, proclaim liberty to the captives and the opening of the prison to those who are bound. He must proclaim the acceptable year of the Lord that those to whom he ministers may be called "trees of righteousness, the planting of the Lord, that he might be glorified." Like his Master, the pastor must speak as one who has authority. All of this and more, the pastor must be to those over whom the Holy Ghost hath made him overseer.

It is easy to see that this is a task of heroic proportions and one to which those only of heroic molds are called. It is apparent, likewise, that no human power is sufficient for these things. The pastor must know that his sufficiency is not in himself, but in God. With Paul he must be able to say "Christ liveth in Me." And out of that blessed fact there must come a purity, a power, and a zeal that will identify him to his people as one sent of God. The pastor must ever bear in mind that out of his heart are the issues of his ministry, and that it is only by the Spirit of God working in him that he will ever be able to edify saints and save sinners.

This sort of an understanding of the ministry will lead to a very definite and a very comprehensive pastoral program.

1. It will be marked by earnestness.

A lightminded, lighthearted attitude toward the ministry pleases neither God nor man. When the saving of souls, the moulding of character, and the shaping of human destiny are at stake, there is no place for cold zeal. It is then, if ever, that the fire of earnest devotion must flame upon the altar of the soul. The earnestness of the great Preacher broke up the fountains of his heart, and made him weap over the recrant city.

2. It will be a busy program.

The pastor who properly shepherds his flock will have neither idle time, nor time for many other things. His problem will be to find days and nights long enough for his work. When Dr. J. H. Jowett, perhaps the greatest of modern preachers, went to New York City to be pastor of Fifth Avenue Presbyterian Church, he knew that he would have many invitations to participate in many things; but preaching, he said, was his business, and he was determined not to be sidetracked from it. This must be so with every pastor. The great Preacher was a man of one goal, and he pressed constantly and tirelessly toward it, and finally said, "I have finished the work which thou gavest me to do."

3. It will be a studious program.

His people will be his ever new and fascinating text book. He will study his folks—their names, aims, problems, hopes and asperations. He will lift up his eyes and look upon the field that he may know where and how to labor that the largest harvests may be garnered for God.

4. It will be a self-growing program.

The pastor never gets grown. He never comes to the full measure of mental and spiritual stature. As a good minister of Jesus Christ, and a workman that needeth not to be ashamed, he must be constantly adding to his mental and spiritual equipment. Success ends where preparation stops. The pastor who does not have a self-growing program will soon have no program at all.

5. It will be a scriptural program.

The great Preacher came to seek and to save that which was lost, and to teach the saved how to live the holy life. That likewise must be the program of every pastor whom he calls to finish that which he began. The faithful pastor will, therefore, call sinners to repentance, and saints to holy living. He will warn of an awful doom that awaits the unrepentant, and encourage saints with the assurance of a final reward. Jesus came seeking. The pastor who rightly senses the scriptural purpose of his mission will greatly magnify the seeking function of the church, and will keep evangelism and holy living strong in his heart and in his ministry fifty-two weeks in the year.

We humbly acknowledge our deep gratitude of God for the faithful preachers whom he calls into his service, and we devoutly pray that they will constantly strive to be good ministers of Jesus Christ.

S. W. TAYLOR,
W. H. NEESE.

(BB) REPORT OF THE COMMITTEE ON CHRISTIAN EDUCATION ·

Your Committee on Christian Education submits the following report for your consideration:

The committee feels that the pastors of our churches and the leaders in the educational work in our local churches need to give careful consideration to the objectives of Christian Education. It is evident that there are many who have a misapprehension as to the real purpose of Christian Education. Life is growth. If that growth is to lead toward a fuller life it must be enriched through a new understanding of worthwhile values. These values are imported through a process which we call education. Education becomes Christian when the stress is placed upon Christian values. The values which are stressed by Christian Education are: 1. God as a reality in human experience; 2. The personality, life and teachings of Jesus; 3. Christlike character; 4. A Christian social order which embodies the ideal of the fatherhood of God and brotherhood of men; 5. A Christian church; 6. The Christian interpretation of life and the universe; and 7. The Bible and other religious experiences of the race.

These main objectives of Christian Education stand before the church today as a great challenge. When we see on every hand so much that is superficial and then come to realize the real mission of the church in the world today, we can appreciate the importance of imparting these ideals to the children, youth and adults of our churches.

It is important that Christian Education do more than lead individuals to know and appreciate these values. It is also the purpose of this program of the church to lead the individual to a fuller acceptance of a complete dedication of his life to a realization of these aims. Without this the whole process will become mechanical, empty and void of any worthwhile results. Therefore we must conclude that Christian Education and the program of evangelism should run hand in hand. We must train to enlist, and after the enlistment we must continue to train in order that the life may grow in the richness and fullness of Christian experience. Educating for Christian living touches all phases of human life, therefore it is necessary that we consider some of the important issues that need to be taken into consideration. Personal religious living needs to receive careful consideration. The religious life begins within the life of the individual, therefore let us stress in the Christian Education program, prayer, meditation, and the ethical ideals which will lead to a well-rounded personality. The committee also feels that these other issues need to be included in the program of Christian Education: economic, industrial and social and racial justice. We believe there is nothing that will do more to break down barriers to these causes than a genuine educational program.

Another item that we stress especially is Christian Education for Temperance. A large number of politicians, newspapers, magazines, business organizations, etc., are saying to us "give us liquor." They are wanting it for social prestige; they desire it for revenue; they demand it for the cause of temperance itself. Our church opposes any such stand. This committee is of the opinion that one of the best methods we have of combatting this evil is temperance education in all of the educational agencies of the church. In addition, we go on record as approving and urging—we will even use stronger language—we request that temperance education be included in the curriculum of the schools of North Carolina.

There are various agencies that need to be awakened to the importance of the Christian educational program: First, we would mention the home. In years past it was a mighty force for Christian living. We believe the secret of its success is found in the fact that the parents, especially the mother, found time to give religious and moral instruction. We call upon the Methodist Protestant homes in North Carolina to spend more time in teaching and training the children in the home along these lines. Second, in the church itself there are a number of organizations that have been established for the purpose of educating the people, namely, classes, clubs, societies and the Sunday School itself. There is all too often a tendency to make these social, money-raising organizations. Our churches are urged to have these organizations meet their real aim in the general program of the church, which is, above everything else, educational.

The North Carolina Conference is fortunate in having within its boundaries High Point College. High Point College has made a real contribution to the church in our state. In addition, it has influenced the educational, business, social, political and civic life of our state. Considering these facts, your committee recommends that this Conference give fuller cooperation to the college in its program.

We feel that recognition should be given to the fine work that is being done for the North Carolina Conference by the Westminster Theological Seminary. It has had a real influence through its training of our ministers for leadership. Because of the scholarship and high type of Christian character of the faculty and its denominational background, we recommend it to the young men of this Conference for their patronage.

Literature plays an important part in shaping the thinking and character of people. We deplore the fact that there are so many cheap, vile, contaminating magazines and newspapers on sale in our cities, towns and villages today. We go on record as urging our pastors and members to use every effort to combat this deplorable situation. One of the means we have of combatting this evil is through the good literature that is available. We call to your attention especially the *Methodist Protestant-Recorder*, the *Methodist Protestant Herald*, the *Missionary Record* and our Sunday School periodicals. In addition we have other high type Christian literature of interdenominational character which should find its way to a number of our homes. We mention the *Christian Herald*, the *International Journal of Religious Education* and the *Christian Century*.

In conclusion we would say that these are only some of the more important facts that have been called to your attention. They contain a real challenge. Brethren, as we go home, let us go into action for a fuller and richer program of Christian Education in the home, in the church, and in all other church-related agencies.

T. J. WHITEHEAD, Chairman
LILLIE MAE BRAXTON, Secretary
J. ELWOOD CARROLL
L. S. NEVILLE
MRS. H. W. MITCHELL.

ANNUAL REPORT OF THE TREASURER OF THE COUNCIL OF RELIGIOUS EDUCATION

November 9, 1936

Number of Sunday Schools paying their apportionment........ 75
Number of Christian Endeavor Societies 25

Total Cash Receipts ....$ 208.87

$ 208.87

Disbursements
Paid to M. P. Herald ....$ 100.00
Council expenses, L. T. S. Schools, etc. 90.88

Total Disbursements 190.88

By Balance Nov. 9th. 1936 .... $ .17.99

Respectfully submitted,

J. CLYDE AUMAN, Treas.

(CC) REPORT OF THE BOARD OF EDUCATION OF THE METHODIST PROTESTANT CHURCH IN NORTH CAROLINA, INCORPORATION, AS OF NOVEMBER 1, 1936

Assets
Deposited with Wachovia Bank & Tr. Co. $ 64.68
Mortgage Vs. Annuity Bonds 1,450.00
Building plans 1,750.00

$ 3,264.68

Real Estate—Greensboro
Real Estate—Greensboro 4,500.00
Lots—Asheboro Street ....————$ 4,500.00

	$610,531.75	
Depreciation	39,252.75	
		$571,249.00

Real Estate—Children's Home

Site	$110,000.00	
Building & Equipment	147,445.00	
		$257,445.00

Furnishings

Robert's Hall	$ 32,589.86	
Dormitories	19,166.55	
Gymnasium	1,000.00	
	$ 62,756.41	
Depreciation	13,189.11	
		$ 39,567.30

l Assets		$876,025.98

Liabilities

Annuity Bonds	1,400.00	
Bonds Outstanding	53,200.00	
Notes Payable Jefferson St. L. Ins. Co.		
Special Loan	19,450.00	
Original Loan	111,482.32	
C. C. Robbins	4,972.58	
J. S. Prickett	4,972.58	
Sundry Notes	112,600.00	
Interest on Bonds	13,000.000	
Due High Point College	32,851.52	

l Liabilities		$253,929.00

:ts over Liabilities		$662,096,98

:ts over Liabilities with Children's Home Property Deducted		$364,651.98

Respectfully Submitted,

C. R. HINSHAW,
Secretary-Treasurer.

(DD) REPORT OF LAYMEN'S MEETING

At a meeting of the Laymen held in Albemarle Methodist Protestant Church on November 7, 1936, the following recommendations were offered and adopted: Believing that the indebtedness of the Methodist Protestant Church of North Carolina incurred by the various Boards at different times over a period of years is 'proving burdensome and is retarding the best interest of our church and should be paid as rapidly as possible, and recognizing the importance of enlisting the sympathy and wholehearted support of our people, and being willing and anxious to aid in this matter, we, the laymen of the N. C. Conference therefore recommend to the Conference that during the period set aside by the President for raising the Annual Conference Debt, each pastor be requested and urged to explain in detail just what the Annual Conference Debt Budget is and the importance of providing funds for the retirement of said debts as rapidly as possible.

We further recommend that the pastor of each charge appoint some one in each local church to assist him in collecting in full the assessment of each church as handed down by the Annual Conference. We further recommend that the President use space in our Church Herald to keep this matter before our people during the period designated for collecting Annual Conference Debt Budget. As laymen we pledge our enthusiastic support and cooperation to the end that our honest obligations may be discharged in full.

We further recommend that no Board of this Conference increase its financial obligations without first submitting the matter to the President of this Conference and his advisory committee.

Committee:

W. A. DAVIES
MRS. B. J. GREGSON
L. W. CAUSEY.

This report was read and adopted at a meeting of the laymen of the North Carolina Conference, November 7, 1936.

L. L. WREN, Chairman,
MRS. JAMES T. BOWMAN,
Secretary.

(EE) REPORT OF ANNUAL CONFERENCE TREASURER

Annual Conference Expense

Receipts:

Balance ....$ 113.93
From charges 3,411.43
————$3,525.36

Disbursements:

Treasurer's Bond ....$ 12.50
Postage 32.48
President's Salary and Expense ......:............... 2,750.00
C. W. Bates, Balance Journals ....:............ 251.40
M. P. Herald 200.00
C. W. Bates, Secretary, Salary 100.00
E. G. Cowan, Statistician, Salary 25.00

J. L. Trollinger, Reporter, Salary...................... 25.00
C. W. Bates, Secretary, Expense........................ 12.28
J. L. Trollinger, Reporter, Expense.................... 12.20
J. H. Allen, Treasurer, Salary............................. 100.00
G. H. Hendry, Fraternal Messenger...................... 4.50
————$3,525.36

World Service

Receipts:
From ·Charges $2,664.62
Disbursements:
Returned Checks ....$ 50.80
Bronna Apple, Treas., N. C. Branch................ 10.00
H. C. Staley, Treasurer 2,603.82
————$2,664.62

Church Extension

Receipts:
Balance ....$ 56.69
From Charges 1,060.32
————$1,117.01
Disbursements:
W. L. Ward, Treasurer $1,117.01

Superannuates

Receipts:
From Charges $1,454.78
Disbursements:
J. Norman Wills, Treasurer $1,454.78

College

Receipts:
From Charges $2,296.68
Disbursements:
Returned Checks ....$ 14.40
High Point College 1,931.47
————$1,945.87

Balance ....$ 350.81

Annual Conference Debt

Receipts:
Balance ....$ 170.46
From Charges 566.11
————$ 736.57
Disbursements:
Returned Checks ....$ 60.00
Interest 18.00
N. M. Harrison—Note 300.00
————$ 378.00

Balance ....$ 358.57

J. H. ALLEN, Treasurer.

SECRETARY'S NOTE.—This report was audited and found correct
by Brothers E. L. Somers and C. J. Roberts, members of our Reids-

ville Church. (This report should have been printed in the 1935 Journal but was delayed in reaching the printer.)

(FF)   MINISTERS MUTUAL PENSION ASSOCIATION

For your consideration we are submitting the following plan for the building of a superannuate fund which is to be separate from yet a supplement to the fund we now have. Payments to this fund are to be made by the ministerial members of this Conference.

1. That pastor's salaries up to $1,500 be assessed 1%.

2. That all salaries above $1,500 be assessed 2%.

3. That the first $500 on all salaries be exempt.

4. That the money for superannuates derived from this source be turned over at each conference to the Conference Board of Superannuates, and that the total amount be distributed each year by them.

5. That pastors be required to report on the conference floor whether or not they have paid their percentage dues to this fund, and if not why not.

6. That the matter of dealing with such pastors be left to the discretion of the Conference.

(GG)   SOCIAL SERVICE

It is the purpose of your committee to discover any evidences of progress, to set forth clearly the present problems confronting our social order, and to suggest a possible solution for existing conditions.

We are gratified at certain signs of progress made. For instance, there has been a moderate improvement of the moving picture industry. Character forming agencies have been established in communities for the purpose of guiding youth into right relationships of life. Economic measures have been passed in order to relieve the oppressed and the poverty stricken. Likewise, a greater interest is being manifested in behalf of the preaching of the gospel.

Certain problems claiming our attention are:

1. Perhaps the first, and that which lies at the bottom of all problems, is the desecration of the Lord's Day. We are aware that when a people cease to properly respect the Sabbath, they begin to lose in spiritual things. Something ought to be done to cause people to keep the Sabbath.

2. An alarming evil today is divorce. It has been brought on by too hasty contracts, the lack of the proper regard for the sacredness of the marriage vows and the true basis of happy home life. Many times children are hindered by handicaps caused by fussing and separated parents. More uniform marriage laws and more stringent measures for regulating divorces would help this situation.

3. Child labor is another problem. Already the best people have recognized this evil as an injustice to the young in forcing them to work before they have sufficiently developed physically and mentally. It is not right for mature persons to be surplanted by children in order to have place for cheaper labor.

4. Liquor has been and continues to be an enemy of humanity. It is not only harmful to the drinker, but to the dependents and society at large. The so-called moderate or occasional drinker is a greater menace to youth than the habitual drinker. Repeal has not improved conditions, but rather, bootlegging, drunkenness, poverty, prostitution and death have alarmingly increased. We should emphatically oppose this monster,—strong drink.

5. Another evil is war. War is contrary to the spirit of the Prince of Peace. The same attitude that breeds or prompts war continues afterwards in a more aggrevated sense. War is a waste of both men and materials, for only untold misery and destruction come from it. War must be outlawed and the principles of peace established.

6. Moving Pictures and the theater are, perhaps, here to stay. What might be a great force for good has been neglected and corrupted by indecency. Careful censorship should be exercised in order to eradicate the objectionable features.

7. Propaganda in the form of alluring advertisement of liquor, cigarettes, etc., are attracting our youth today. · Such suggestions deceive the young minds, and cause bad habits to be formed which are of great harm to the victims.

8. Gambling, whether on a small or large scale, is not a Christian practice. Games of chance, betting, etc., should not be tolerated.

9. What many regard as perhaps as harmful things, others look upon as detrimental. We refer to dancing, card playing, beer drinking, gossip and gathering at road houses. If such practices are doubtful and harmful to some devout Christians it seems that others ought to refrain, as Paul tells us, in order not to offend.

What can be done to solve these problems?

1. Regular attendance at church services will help considerably. A prominent judge of this State has challenged persons coming before him as criminals in fifty court houses, that if they could prove regular attendance at Sunday school he would remit the penalty. But no one has accepted the challenge. This proves the value of church attendance.

2. A regular study of the Bible and good literature will aid greatly in correcting the faults of our social relationships. Conduct is founded largely by what we read and digest mentally.

3. A more emphatic preaching of the gospel as the power of God unto salvation of the individual and society is needed. The time has come for this emphasis, and the people will respond to the Gospel messages.

4. Finally, prayer will be used as the force for awakening the mind and quickening the soul for nobler Christian living. What these other methods will do partically, or fail to do, prayer will accomplish by the assistance of God.

The Committee.

(HH)   COMMITTEE ON BLANKET INSURANCE

We, your Committee on Blanket Insurance, beg to report that thirty-eight applications were received for insurance under the plan as approved at the 1935 Conference. Fifty applications were required to put the policy in force. Before the remaining twelve could be secured, several of the applications advanced to the non-insurable age. So little interest in insurance was manifest by the brethren of the Conference, we suggest that the matter be dropped and the duties of the Committee terminate with this report.

Respectfully Submitted,

N. M. HARRISON,
GEO. R. BROWN,
R. C. STUBBINS.

(II)   REPORT OF COMMITTEE ON WORK OF REV. J. S. WILLIAMS, D.D.

Whereas, Rev. J. S. Williams, D.D., Chaplain of the Mission of the Good Samaritan, Asheville, is closing his 25th year in that position,

Therefore: Be it resolved, that the Conference go on record as expressing its appreciation for the service Brother Williams has rendered through the years to the sick and suffering ones to whom he has ministered so faithfully, and

Be it resolved, that we extend to Dr. Williams our hope that he will be spared for many years to carry on his blessed ministry.

Further, that a copy of these resolutions be sent to Brother Williams and printed in both the Conference Journal and the *Methodist Protestant Herald.*

T. M. JOHNSON, Chairman,
J. N. WILLS,
C. W. BATES, Secretary.

(JJ)   REPORT OF CONFERENCE COUNCIL OF RELIGIOUS EDUCATION

The Executive Committee of the Conference Council of Religious Education submits the report of the activities of the Council for the past year.

Young People's Day was observed during the months of January and February, and although weather conditions cut the attendance down considerable, the response in the offerings was especially good. We shall be glad when all churches in our Conference lay stress on this phase of our work. The number of churches observing this day is growing, but there are still many that do not cooperate.

During the month of March this year a series of Leadership Education schools was conducted by Rev. J. Elwood Carroll. Interest in this very important part of our program is also growing but we need the cooperation of every pastor in our Conference. Three schools were conducted in March with a total enrollment of 191. 12 courses were offered in the First Series and 12 in the Second Series.

The annual Leadership Education School was held at High Point College in June, with a total enrollment of 142. New features in this school this year were a demonstration Vacation Church School, discussion groups, and addressed by outstanding speakers in our State. A course in Missions was offered by Miss Bettie Brittingham. The students who came this year seemed to be of a higher type than usual and this school was considered one of the best, if not the best, in our history.

The Conference Council sponsored a large number of Vacation Church Schools, the total enrollment being 669, with 449 certificates issued. One school with an enrollment of 36 was held for one week only, the others were of two weeks duration. We should like to remind the pastors that this phase of our work is absolutely essential to the training of the children in our churches and we shall be glad to help any who call upon us.

Special mention should be made of the work being done in the department of Music and Art under the direction of Rev. E. L. Ballard. A radio program was given during the summer Leadership Education School. The evening given to this department for chorus work is growing in interest each year. The director of this department is also trying to help a number of churches to raise their appreciation for a better type of music and the efforts are seemingly fruitful.

We again want to thank the editor of the *Methodist Protestant Herald* for the generous space given us in the *Herald*.

Each year we see evidences of growth and progress in our work and we are calling upon pastors and people to give their cooperation and support to our undertakings.

The following recommendations are submitted as a program of action for the following year:

1. Leadership Education Program. This will be under the supervision of the vice-president of the Council, Rev. J. Elwood Carroll, who is director of Leadership Education.

    A. That the pastors hold classes in their local churches, using First and Second Series courses.

    B. That area Leadership Education Schools be held as they were last year, but not in the same places.

    C. That the annual Leadership Education School be held at High Point College and that the dates be June 21-26, which will be the week following the third Sunday.

2. That the pastors be requested to place special emphasis on Vacation Church Schools in their churches, and that they cooperate with the Superintendents of Sunday Schools in this phase of the program.

4. That special attention be paid to the Youth Program "Christian Youth Building a New World," and a special effort be made to bring this program before the people in all of our churches.

5. That the Conference pledge its support to the total program of Christian Education and the Department of Religious Education of our denomination.

6. That the same plan of financing the work of the Council be continued.

Respectfully Submitted,

T. J. WHITEHEAD, President,
MRS. E. L. BALLARD,
Secretary.

(KK)   REPORT ON COMMITTEE ON STEWARDSHIP

Your Committee on Stewardship has received the following paragraph from the recent annual message of our president. It reads as follows:

"There are, I suppose, just a few churches in our entire conference which have a working system for raising their finances. Just why so many otherwise reasonable men and women shy at a system for raising the money necessary to pay their pastor and their Conference claims, I have failed to understand. We have pastoral charges the percapita contribution to all claims which is two dollars; others paying fifteen times that amount, or thirty dollars, and the difference in the per capita contributions is in methods in raising these claims. Our church ranks quite low in per capita contributions when compared to other denominations. It surely is not because we are poorer than most of them. The reason must be found elsewhere, and we trace it to the lack of proper methods in raising our claims. Presupposing that our members are regenerated when they join our church, and that the pastor has properly impressed upon them when they join what they are pledging to it their financial support, we are persuaded that a properly organized and wisely worked financial plan in our churches would secure larger contributions to all claims. There is absolutely no substitute for it."

Accordingly, we recommend that the Conference take these words seriously and make an honest, sincere attempt to accept and work out these wise suggestions. Also, we commend those churches which have instituted the envelope system during the past year. Further, we commend those churches which have made special attempts to encourage tithing during the year. These are all steps in the right direction.

Respectfully Submitted,

H. F. FOGLEMAN,
N. G. BETHEA,
J. G. ROGERS.

(LL)   SECRETARY'S EXPENSE ACCOUNT

Receipts

J. H. Allen, Treasurer	$234.50
Sale of Journals	227.30
25% Payment North Carolina Bank	5.14
	———$ 461.80

Disbursements

Stockton Press	$428.00
Postage	5.25
Service Charge	3.00
Envelopes (Official Blanks)	.85
Binding Quadrennial Journals	2.50
Carbon Paper, Ribbon	1.62
Conference Stationery	2.16
McCulloch and Swain, Programs, Paper	9.00
Ordination Bibles and Credentials	9.50
	———$ 461.80

C. W. BATES, Secretary.

Number Members	963	1,009	46	....
Number Church Papers Taken	1,788	1,799	10	....

FINANCIAL

Promised Pastors	$ 85,152	$ 89,098	$ 3,946	$.............
Paid Pastors	81,260	88,467	7,207	....
Promised Next Year	85,152	89,098	3,946	....
Paid on Church Buildings	14,774	12,781	....	1,993
Paid on Church Debt	10,090	16,433	6,343	....
Paid on Church Interest	9,805	6,469	....	3,336
Paid on Church Improvement	10,248	13,761	3,513	....
Paid on Parsonage Building	4,505	654	....	3,851
Paid on Parsonage Improvements	2,614	4,149	1,535	....
Paid on Parsonage Debt	2,416	3,906	1,490	....
Paid on Parsonage Interest	798	696	....	102
Raised by Sunday Schools	20,581	20,777	196	....
Raised by Woman's Auxiliary for Local Work	11,335	11,009	....	326
Raised by C. E. Societies	1,299	1,222	....	77
Raised by Sunday Schools for Children's Home	9,273	10,030	757	....
Raised for Current Expense	21,620	20,777	....	843
Raised for Total Local Interest	188,288	204,564	15,756	....
Grand Total Raised	218,496	263,094	54,598	....

GENERAL AND ANNUAL CONFERENCE BUDGETS

Paid by Membership Direct	$ 1,103	$ 1,020	$	$ 83
Paid by Young People's Day	407	328	....	79
Paid by Easter Offering	406	468	62	....
Paid by Children's Day	409	634	225	....
Paid by Rally Day	272	382	110	....
Paid by Special Offerings	232	227	....	5
Paid by Woman's Auxiliary for World Service	4,893	4,979	86	....
Total for World Service	7,707	7,978	271	....
Paid for Conference Expense	2,830	3,000	1,170	....
Paid for Conference Debt	1,070	1,207	137	....
Paid for Church Extension	1,112	1,130	18	....
Paid for Superannuates	1,492	1,915	423	....
Paid by Woman's Auxiliary for N. C. Work	2,573	2,694	121	....
Total for Annual Conference Claims	9,521	10,159	638	....
Paid for High Point College	3,011	3,051	40	....
Paid for Herald Subsidy	451	425	....	26
Paid for Religious Education	233	210	....	23
Other Conference Interests	12,466	13,761	1,295	....

VALUE OF CHURCH PROPERTY 1936

	1935	1936	Incr.	Decr.
Value of Churches	$1,533,650	$1,418,900 $	....	$114,750
Present Church Indebtedness	182,411	165,941	....	16,470
Churches Insured for	449,555	441,150	....	8,405
Other Church Property	28,250	6,373	....	22,877
Value of Parsonages	219,800	216,000	....	3,800
Present Indebtedness	21,568	16,936	....	3,632
Insured for	90,500	98,520	8,020	....
Value of Children's Home Property	257,400	272,400	15,000	....
Value of High Point College	645,633	720,633	75,000	....
Value of All Church Property	3,276,696	2,634,306	....	642,690

E. G. COWAN, Statistical Secretary.

Seagrove, N. C.

(NN)   REPORT ON COMMITTEE ON OFFICIALS CHARACTER

We your Committee on Official Character submits the following report:

We recommend that the Official Character of all the ministers and preachers of the Conference be passed.

T. M. JOHNSON, Chairman,
GEO. R. BROWN.

(OO)   CONFERENCE TREASURER'S REPORT

1935

Annual Conference Expense

Receipts:

Balance	$ 113.93	
From charges	3,411.43	
		$3,525.36

Disbursements:

Treasurer's Bond	$ 12.50
Postage	32.48
President's Salary and Expense	2,750.00
C. W. Bates, Balance Journals	251.40
M. P. Herald	200.00
C. W. Bates, Secretary, Salary	100.00
E. G. Cowan, Statistician, Salary	25.00
J. L. Trollinger, Reporter, Salary	25.00
C. W. Bates, Secretary, Expense	12.28
J. L. Trollinger, Reporter, Expense	12.20
J. H. Allen, Treasurer, Salary	100.00
G. H. Hendry, Fraternal Messenger	4.50
	$3,525.36

World Service

Receipts:

From Charges	$2,664.62

Disbursements:

Returned Checks	$ 50.80
Bronna Apple, Treas., N. C. Branch	10.00
H. C. Staley, Treasurer	2,603.82
	$2,664.62

From Charges 1,060.32
                 —————$1,117.01

Disbursements:
W. L. Ward, Treasurer 1,117.01

Superannuates

Receipts:
From Charges $1,454.78
Disbursements:
J. Norman Wills, Treasurer 1,454.78

College

Receipts:
From Charges $2,296.68
Disbursements:
Returned Checks ....$ 14.40
High Point College 1,931.47
               —————$1,945.87

Balance .... $ 350.81

Annual Conference Debt

Receipts:
Balance ....$ 170.46
From Charges ....: 566.11
               —————$ 736.57

Disbursements:
Returned Checks ....$ 60.00
Interest 18.00
N. M. Harrison—Note 300.00
               —————$ 3,78.00

Balance .... $ 358.57

J. H. ALLEN, Treasurer.

SECRETARY'S NOTE.—This report was audited and found correct by Brothers E. L. Somers and C. J. Roberts, members of our Reidsville Church. (*This report should have been printed in the 1935 Journal but was delayed in reaching the printer.*)

CONFERENCE TREASURER'S REPORT
1936

Annual Conference Expense

Receipts:
From Charges $3,521.13
Disbursements:
Treasurer's Receipt Blanks ....$ 6.50
Treasurer's Bond 12.50
Postage 16.24
President's Salary and Expense 2,750.00
C. W. Bates on Journals 225.00

M. P. Herald	200.00
M. P. Herald, Subsidy	2.50
C. W. Bates, Salary	100.00
C. W. Bates, Annual Conference Expense	18.50
E. G. Cowan, Statistician Salary	25.00
E. G. Cowan, Expense	.75
J. L. Trollinger, Reporter, Salary	25.00
J. L. Trollinger, Reporter Expense	7.75
J. H. Allen, Treasurer, Salary	100.00
Returned Checks	12.00

$3,501.74

Balance .... $ 19.39

World Service Budget

Receipts:
From Charges $2,658.59
Disbursements:
Returned Checks 20.00
H. C. Staley, Treas. 2,638.59

$2,658.59

Annual Conference Debt

Receipts:
Balance 358.57
From Charges 1,135.25

$1,493.82

Disbursements:
Interest 180.00
On Lewis Note 500.00
F. R. Stout, Parsonage Trustee 768.57
Returned checks 5.00

$1,453.57

Balance .... $ 40.25

Church Extension

Receipts:
From Charges $1,053.36
Disbursements:
Returned Checks 15.00
W. L. Ward, Treas. 1,038.36

$1,053.36

Superannuates

Receipts:
From Charges $1,793.27

Disbursements:
Returned Checks 20.00
J. Norman Wills, Treasurer 1,773.27

$1,793.27

Returned checks 5.00

$2,555.81

Balance .... $ 269.29

J. H. ALLEN, Treasurer.

Auditor's Report

Your committee appointed by the Conference to audit the accounts of J. H. Allen, Conference Treasure, beg to submit the following report:

We have carefully examined and checked all items received and disbursed by him and find them to be correct.

E. L. SOMERS
CHAS. J. ROBERTS

(PP)   REPORT OF NOMINATING COMMITTEE

Committee on Religious Education—J. Clyde Auman, J. E. Carroll, George R. Brown, N. G. Bethea, R. C. Stubbins.

Committee on Evangelism—F. W. Paschall, L. E. Mabry, A. D. Shelton, G. H. Hendry, E. A. Cook.

Committee Advisory to President—A. G. Dixon, J. D. Williams, J. C. Madison, R. C. Stubbins, F. W. Paschall.

Committee on Rural Church—J. W. Braxton, J. T. Bowman, G. L. Curry, C. B. Baskett, Wilberforce Causey.

United Dry Forces—Edward Suits, Dr. J. A. Pickett.

North Carolina Council of Churches—P. E. Lindley, N. G. Bethea, F. W. Paschall.

Members of Southern Interracial Committee—J. C. Madison, J. E. Carroll.

To Audit Treasurer's Book—E. L. Somers, C. J. Roberts.

Fraternal Messengers—
    Blue Ridge-Atlantic M. E.—J. E. Carroll
    North Carolina M. E., South—T. J. Whitehead
    Western North Carolina, M. E. South—C. W. Bates

To Preach Conference Sermon—C. E. Ridge.

To Preach Ordinaion Sermon—P. S. Kennett.

Nominating Committee—E. O. Peeler, E. A. Bingham, C. G. Isley.

Conference Trustees—W. F. Ashburn, J. Norman Wills—1940.

Boundary Committee—R. M. Andrews, Edward Suits—1940.

Board of Church Extension—W. A. Davies, W. F. Redding, Jr. —1940.

Annual Conference Council of Religious Education—P. E. Lindley—1940.

Committee on Methodist Cooperation—W. T. Hanner, R. M. Andrews.

College Trustees—J. E. Pritchard, R. M. Cox, Dr. J. H. Cutchin, W. L. Hunsucker.

Director of Pastors' Summer School—S. W. Taylor.

Trustees District Parsonage—J. Norman Wills, J. M. Millikan, F. R. Stout, W. T. Hanner.

Committee on Financial Recommendations—R. M. Andrews, G. I. Humphries, J. E. Pritchard, A. G. Dixon, T. M. Johnson, T. J. Whitehead, W. L. Ward.

Conference Committee on Stewardship—N. G. Bethea, George R. Brown, J. G. Rogers.

College Committee of Ten—Ms. D. S. Coltrane, Mrs. M. A. Coble, Mrs. J. H. Cutchin, L. F. Ross, A. J. Koonce, J. T. Warlick, Revs. J. E. Pritchard, C. E. Ridge, H. F. Surratt, B. M. Williams.

H. F. FOGLEMAN,
H. L. ISLEY,
J. F. MINNIS.

(QQ)   REPORT OF COMMITTEE ON FRATERNAL RELATIONS

Your Committee on Fraternal Relations respectfully submits the following report: It is with pleasure we extend to Rev. C. G. Isley, pastor, First Methodist Protestant Church, Albemarle and members our sincere gratitude and appreciation for the hospitable manner in which we have been entertained. Also to Rev. W. D. Reed and the people of Friendship Church, and the people of Porter Church and to the many families of Albemarle, and adjoining communities of other faiths, who have helped to entertain this our annual session of North Carolina Annual Conference.

We wish to extend our sincere thanks to the local paper, *The Stanley News,* and to the associated press for the favorable publicity that we have received during this session of our annual conference.

We are grateful to the ministers of the city and surrounding communities for opening their churches to us.

It has been our pleasure to extend the courtesies of the Conference to visiting friends, both of our own church and of other denominations.

Recommendation: That the Program Committee of the annual conference make provision, in their program for the presentation of visiting friends.

Respectfully submitted,

E. O. PEELER, Chairman,
K. G. HOLT, Secretary.

(RR) REPORT OF THE STATIONING COMMITTEE

First District

G. L. Curry, Chairman

Creswell—O. L. Easter
Chase City—To be supplied
Enfield—D. R. Williams
Greenville—J. M. Morgan
Halifax—W. M. Howard, Jr.
Littleton—J. H. Trolinger
Spring Church—G. L. Curry
Whitakers—D. R. Williams

Second District

T. J. Whitehead, Chairman

Granville—C. L. Spencer
Henderson—T. J. Whitehead
Vance—J. D. Cranford

Third District

E. A. Bingham, Chairman

Alamance—H. L. Isley
Orange—H. F. Fogleman
Mebane—D. I. Garmer
Saxapahaw—E. A. Bingham

Fourth District

F. W. Paschall, Chairman

Burlington—F. W. Paschall
Fountain Place—R. E. L. Moser
Gibsonville—R. C. Stubbins
Glen Raven—R. S. Troxler
Graham—H. F. Surratt

Fifth District

F. E. Carroll, Chairman

Greensboro:
Calvary—J. E. Pritchard
Grace—J. E. Carroll
St. Paul—A. D. Shelton
West End—N. G. Bethea
Midway—J. E. Garlington
Moriah—Leo Pittard
Shady Grove—to be supplied
Tabernacle—E. A. Lamb

Sixth District

G. R. Brown, Chairman

Brown Summit—Leo Pittard
Danville—C. P. Morris
Draper—J. L. Love
Flat Rock—J. A. Burgess
Haw River—C. W. Bates
Reidsville—G. R. Brown

Seventh District

J. W. Braxton, Chairman

Chatham—A. Q. Lindley
Liberty—A. M. Smith
Mt. Pleasant—J. W. Braxton
Mt. Hermon—J. R. Anderson
Siler City—A. M. Smith

Eighth District

S. W. Taylor, Chairman

Asheboro—S. W. Taylor
Richland—M. C. Henderson
Randleman—J. B. Trogdon
Seagrove-Love Joy—
　　　　　　　E. G. Cowan
Why Not—C. H. Hill
Randolph—G. L. Reynolds

Ninth District

J. C. Madison, Chairman

Guilford—C. B. Way
High Point:
First—J. C. Madison
Lebanon—J. R. Hutton
Welch Memorial—
　　　　　　J. D. Williams
Rankin Memorial—
　　　　　　Edward Suits

Tenth District

J. C. Auman, Chairman

Mt. Zion—E. P. Hamilton
N. Davidson—W. H. Neese
Thomasville:
Community—J. C. Auman
First—O. C. Loy
Pleasant Grove—F. R. Love

Eleventh District

C. E. Ridge—Chairman

Lexington:
First—L. E. Mabry
State Street—J. P. Pegg
Shiloh—C. E. Ridge
Spencer—To be supplied
Mocksville—R. L. Hethcox

Twelfth District

J. T. Bowman, Chairman

Davidson—C. L. Grant
Mt. Ebal—J. T. Bowman
Denton—J. T. Bowman

Thirteenth District

J. L. Trollinger, Chairman

Forsyth—R. A. Hunter
W. Forsyth—G. B. Ferree
Pinnacle—J. D. Morris
Winston, First—J. L. Trollinger

Fourteenth District

T. G. Madison, Chairman

Bess Chapel—To be supplied
Bessemer City—To be supplied
Shelby-Caroleen—L. S. Helms
Connelly Springs
          —Herman Yokeley
Cleveland—T. G. Madison
Lincolnton—W. L. Harkey
Fallston—B. M. Williams
Fairfield—W. L. Harkey

Fifteenth District

C. G. Isley, Chairman

Roberta—E. A. Cook
Midland—E. A. Cook

Concord—E. O. Peeler
Kannapolis—To be supplied
Friendship—R. L. Vickery
Porter—C. G. Isley
Albemarle—C. G. Isley
Pine Bluff—C. G. Isley

Sixteenth District

G. H. Hendry—Chairman

Charlotte—G. H. Hendry.
Mecklenburg—J. R. Short
Rockingham—H. W. Bell

Seventeenth District

T. M. Johnston—Chairman

Anderson—T. M. Johnson
Yarborough—G. K. Holt

Eighteenth District

E. L. Ballard, Chairman

Asheville—E. L. Ballard
Democrat—W. C. Clark
Pensacola—W. C. Clark
Weaverville—W. C. Clark

Left without appointment at own request: D. D. Broome, W. M. Loy, D. T. Huss.

In the hands of the President: P. E. Bingham, Atlas Ridge, Q. L. Joyner.

Honorary Members: S. K. Spahr, G. I. Humphreys.

President Westminster Theological Seminary—C. E. Forlines

Professors in High Point College: P. S. Kenneth, P. E. Lindley

Promotional Secretary of High Point College: N. M. Harrison

Loaned to Mission of Good Samaritan, Asheville: J. S. Williams

Loaned to Board of Missions: J. P. Minnis

Executive Secretary General Conference Council of Religious Education: F. L. Gibbs

Superintendent Bethel Home-Homer Casto

Superintendent Children's Home: A. G. Dixon

President Annual Conference—R. M. Andrews

Editor *Methodist Protestant Herald*—R. M. Andrews

Supernumerary, Richland Charge—W. F. McDowell

Superannuates: W. T. Totten, T. F. McCulloch, W. M. Pike, G. W. Holmes, W. F. Ashburn, H. S. B. Thompson, G. F. Millaway, H. L. Powell, D. D. Reed, T. A. Williams.

(SS)   REPORT OF COMMITTEE ON CONFERENCE PROGRAM

Your Committee considers that the program of the church is included under the following functional phases: 1. Christian Education, 2. Evangelism, 3. Missions and Social Service, 4. The Preacher and Preaching, and 5. Worship. Our purpose has been to set forth the major emphases and recommendations as found in your reports of officers, boards, and committees; and to arrange these under the above listed five major heads.

1. As a means to efficiency a plan for the entire year's program has been called for with specific objectives for each month, and the observance of specified days. (Reports A. D. & G.)

November:
   a. A knowledge of the plan herein stated.
   b. Skeleton outline of your entire year's program, with official endorsement for as much as possible by your first quarterly conference.
   c. Observance of Thanksgiving, including the "Day's Wage" offering for our Children's Home. (G)

December: Raise an offering for the Seminary. (Send to Dr. C. E. Forlines, President, Westminster, Md.)

January-February:
   a. Raise Annual Conference Expense apportionment. (A)
   b. Observe Young People's Day with an offering for Board of Christian Education. (BB)
   c. February Thank Offering for Board of Missions.

March-April:
   a. Raising of High Point College apportionment. (A)
   b. Easter Offering for Board of Missions.
   c. Women attend North Carolina Branch Meeting.

May-June:
   a. Raising of Church Extension apportionment. (A)
   b. Support the annual summer school of Leadership Education. (JJ).
   c. Ministers attend Extension School at High Point and summer school at Duke University. (Z)

July-August:
   a. Raising of Annual Conference Debt apportionment. (A)

September-October:
   a. Raising of Superannuate Fund apportionment. (A)
   b. Fall Thank Offering for Board of Christian Education.
   c. Observance of Rally Day, including an offering for Board of Christian Education.

2. Arrange a systematic program for financing your year's church activities (A).

3. Study the unabridged reports of committees, boards, and officers, as adopted by the Conference (A).

4. Development of Young People's choirs (L).

5. Use of public school music teachers to improve church music. (L).

6. The learning of new hymns by having definite periods for that purpose (L).

7. Appoint committee for handling each special day well in advance of the day (M).

8. Subscribe to the church periodicals and Sunday school literature (BB) and as a special effort to procure subscriptions to the *"Herald"* that each pastor appoint a *Herald* agent (V).

9. Adequate nurture of the new convert that he may grow in the beauty of his new Christian character (Y).

10. Pastors to take advantage of any Methodist summer schools for ministers (Z).

11. Pastors and church leaders ought to know and keep in mind the objectives of Christian Education (BB).

12. Christian Education and Evangelism are not antagonistic, but supplemental (BB).

13. Pastors and church leaders ought to know the issues with which they are confronted in a program of Christian Education (BB).

14. As a means of taking inventory there should be an evaluation of the agencies of education such as the home, groups within the church, and our college (BB).

15. As a method of education in a specific project in missions, it is recommended that we study carefully the report of the Superintendent of the Children's Home (G).

16. Study for a knowledge of the issues which we confront as listed in Committee on Social Service (GG).

17. Learn our position on social issues as stated in the report of the Committee on Social Service (GG).

18. Cooperation with the Conference Council program, the local schools, area schools, and Vacation Church Schools (JJ).

II. Evangelism

1. The most important function of the church is soul-saving (Y).

2. There are many methods of Evangelism, such as:

a. Revival meeting.

b. Personal touch.

c. Pastor's instruction class.

d. Period of Evangelistic preaching.

e. Special occasions and days.

f. Pastor's connection with "Won-by-One' Band (Y).

III. Missions and Social Service

1. Missions now in a new age due to various and counter ideas and movements (E).

2. Active and thorough Woman's Auxiliary is a great means to creating a progressive church (E).

3. Thorough study of the selected mission study book is urged (E).

4. As a project in actual social service, raise a gift, collect clothing, can fruit, or clothe a child in the Children's Home (G).

5.   We help ourselves by helping others especially in giving ourselves to the support of a missionary program (M).

6.   Each convert should not only be improved in Christian character, but definitely related to some work of Christian service (Y).

IV.   Preacher and Preaching

1. *The Preacher:*
   a. There is a need for arrangement for care of our retired preachers (A).
   b. Appropriate parsonages for our ministers (I)—First, pastor should take special interest in his home, and, Secondly, he should designate a committee on parsonage improvement and upkeep.
   c. His many duties will demand a definite pastoral program (AA).
   d. He must keep his mind alert by study of books, his people, and the writings of God's Spirit (AA).
   e. The preparation for our ministry ought to be made in our own seminary (BB).
   f. As a means of renewing mental concepts all our ministers ought to attend the Seminary Extension School to be held at High Point College (BB).
   g. Attendance upon the National Preaching Mission at Raleigh, November 27-30, 1936 (F, Y).
   h. We trust that the additional plan for supplementing the Superannuate Fund will prove a success (GG).
   i. The pastor has a complex task, therefore should strive to arise to all occasions of usefulness (AA).

2. *Preaching:*
   a. Participation in National Preaching Mission by preaching in local church or churches is feasible (F, Y).
   b. A minister must be a preacher of the Word (AA).
   c. He must be aflame with the Spirit of God (AA).

V.   Worship

1.   A better atmosphere for worship by beautifying the grounds and buildings (C).

2.   A suitable order of worship. Two sample orders of worship are given in Report C.

3.   The ordinances of Baptism and Holy Communion should be used as means of deepening the spiritual experiences. In order that this may be realized there should be complete and adequate preparation of the material elements, worship program, and understanding on the part of the worshipers (J).

4.   The assistance of good music through the use of substantial song books, preferably the Methodist Hymnal in sufficient quantity for all (L).

5.   Careful selection of hymns by the pastor for church worship, and by the leaders in worship groups directed by laymen such as the Sunday School and Christian Endeavor (L).

6.   A greater emphasis be placed upon congregational hymn singing as a means of fellowship and worship (L).

Recommendations

1. That this report be published in the *Methodist Protestant Herald* this week.

2. That each minister be urged to read this report before his first quarterly conference.

3. That this report be the basis for articles for the *Herald*.

4. That this report be used as the basis of programs for area and district meetings.

5. That the pastors keep this program before them and follow it as much as possible throughout the entire year.

6. That the President check up on the ministers quarterly as to whether they are following this program.

T. J. WHITEHEAD, Chairman,
J. E. CARROLL, Secretary.

RESOLUTION No. 1

WHEREAS, in our system of itinerancy a minister seldom remains on the same charge for many years at a time; whereas the Conference is rather compact, thus frequently placing a minister near his former charge; and whereas some of our ministers have yielded to the desire to revisit former parishioners to the end that friction has been created, or at least a division of loyalty on the part of the laymen visited between their new pastor and their former pastor, therefore,

BE IT RESOLVED, *First*, That this Conference go on record as being opposed to a minister visiting any persons on his former charge without the assurance that the visit is entirely agreeable to the present pastor;

Secondly, That all pastors be called upon to report to the President of the Conference immediately any visit by a former pastor among their parishioners; and

Thirdly, That the President be requested to remind any pastor who visits former members of the disapproval of this Conference of any such act, and that upon a second offense the President be empowered to reprimand, in the presence of two other ministers, such an offender.

J. ELWOOD CARROLL,
J. CLYDE AUMAN.

RESOLUTION No. 2

WHEREAS, the Westminster Theological Seminary, for the last three years, has conducted a Summer School for pastors and preachers of our conference, at High Point College, and

WHEREAS, for the service, we have paid only their bare expenses, and

WHEREAS, but few of our ministers have taken advantage of this opportunity for further equipping themselves for greater work of the pastorate, therefore;

BE IT RESOLVED:

(1) That the Conference hereby express its appreciation to the Seminary for her generosity and for the efficient services of her faculty;

(2) That our pastors be urged to attend the school, whether they be seminary graduates or not, and take advantage of the courses offered;

(3) That the directors of the school, be elected by conference, (see page 9 of 1935 Journal) select a director of the school whose time and interest will permit proper publicizing and building up of the school;

(4) In keeping with the request of the President of the Seminary, that the pastors be requested to take an annual offering during December on his charge as a special contribution to the Seminary.

Respectfully submitted,

GEORGE L. CURRY,
N. M. HARRISON.

RESOLUTION No. 3

Resolved, that it is the sense of this conference that our annual sessions may be shortened to the convenience of both ministers and laymen, and also to the Conference host; and that this can be done without affecting adversely the efficiency of our conference work: Therefore,

Be it Resolved, That our session next year, and all succeeding sessions begin on Thursday morning at 10 o'clock, and close on Monday.

S. W. TAYLOR,
J. L. TROLLINGER.

OVERTURES

1. The Basis of Union.

General Conference action: "Moved that the report of the Commission be received and that the Plan of Union forthwith, upon the adjournment of this General Conference, be sent and transmitted to the several Annual Conferences of this church for action thereon as provided in Article XVII of the Constitution of the Methodist Protestant Church."

General Conference action: (Adopted by a Roll Call vote of 142 for to 29 against.)

Annual Conference action: (Adopted by this Conference 124 for and 26 against.)

2. "Resolved: That there shall be sent down to the Annual Conferences as an overture, the following change in the Constitution:

"Change Article IX, paragraph 3, of the Constitution to read: "'To determine the qualifications and status of the Annual and Mission Conferences and define their boundaries; provided, however, that the Annual Conferences of any two or more districts shall have power, by mutual agreement, to alter their respective adjoining boundaries, or to set off new districts; but every such alteration shall be reported to the ensuing General Conference for its action."

(General Conference action: This resolution was adopted by unanimous vote.)

(Annual Conference action—Adopted.)

OBITUARY

REV. W. F. KENNETT

William Fillmore Kennett, son of J. F. and Mary A. Kennett, was born in Guilford County, N. C., June 18, 1856, and departed this life at Greensboro, N. C., on January 14, 1936, his age being seventy-nine years, six months and twenty-six days. He was converted when a boy of sixteen years at a camp meeting at Tabernacle Methodist Protestant Church. Even before his conversion he felt the call to preach the gospel and after his conversion he was never able to get away from that conviction. He was educated in the schools of his community and at Oak Ridge Institute under those eminent educators, Professors J. Allen and Martin H. Holt. During his school days a friendship sprang up between him and them which lasted as long as the Holts lived.

Brother Kennett was licensed to preach under the pastorate of Rev. J. R. Ball in 1883. At the Annual Conference of 1883, held at Fair Grove Church on the Haw River Circuit, he was assigned to Buncombe Circuit, which charge he served for two years. On May 21, 1885, he was united in marriage to Miss Annie L. Hanner of Chatham County, a woman of fine spiritual attainments, who passed to her reward in 1918. To this union two children were born; one dying at the age of eighteen months while the other is Dr. Paul S. Kennett of High Point College. Brother Kennett was married the second time December 22, 1920, this time to Mrs. Ella Paris of Greensboro, who proved to be a very devoted companion to him in his declining years.

He was elected president of the North Carolina Annual Conference in November, 1899, and served until the close of 1900. He served the church continuously, either as pastor or president from the time he entered in 1883 until November, 1926, when he was superannuated. He was a representative to the General Conference four times, and was a member of many of the important boards in his own conference for many years. The following charges were served by him: Buncombe, Winston-Salem, Orange, Flat Rock, Henderson, Randleman, Pinnacle, Mt. Zion, Mebane, St. Paul, Forsyth, Richland and Granville. He was on the Flat Rock Circuit four different times, serving this charge seventeen years in all, the last pastorate lasting for a period of seven years.

As a preacher he was earnest and studious. He had the happy faculty of being able to speak intelligently on any subject without very much time for preparation. With all his heart he believed in the atoning sacrifice of Jesus Christ, and preached it so long as he was able to preach and then trusted in it to his last day upon the earth. Death did not come as a surprise to him; he looked forward to it and prepared for it, having selected the minister to have charge of his funeral service and having written a brief history of his life in order that the important facts might be easily accessible.

The funeral services were conducted from Hebron Church, near Mebane on January 15, by Rev. J. E. Pritchard, assisted by Rev. R. M. Andrews, W. F. Ashburn and B. M. Williams. His body was then placed beside that of his first wife in the Hebron Church Cemetery. Truly it can be said of him that he fought a good fight and kept the faith.

> "Servant of God, well done,
> Thy glorious warfare's past
> The battle's fought, the victory's won,
> And thou art crowned at last."

In addition to his son and wife he is survived by the following four brothers, J. C., of Julian, J. A., of Concord, J. M., of Mooresville and C. O., of Greensboro; and by four sisters, Mrs. Jane Bergman of Guilford College, Mrs. Nannine Slack of Greensboro, Mrs. W. F. Ivey and Mrs. J. J. Lamb of Randleman.

J. E. PRITCHARD,
W. F. ASHBURN,
J. NORMAN WILLS.

HONOR ROLL

HONOR ROLL OF CHURCHES AND CHARGES

CHARGE OR CHURCH	Pastor's Salary	World Service	A. C. Expense	A. C. Debt	Church Extension	Superannuates	H. P. College	Herald Quota	Herald Subsidy	N. C. C. Rel. Ed.
Alamance:										
Sapling Ridge	*								*	*
Center	*	*	*	*	*	*	*	*	*	*
Bethel	*		*		*	*	*		*	*
Rock Creek									*	*
Anderson:										
Liberty Hill	*		*							
Fairview	*						*			
Asheboro	*	*	*	*	*	*	*		*	*
Asheville								*		
Bess Chapel	*	*								
Bessemer City	*		*	*	*	*				
Brown Summit-Moriah										
Brown Summit	*					*				
Moriah	*					*				
Burlington, First	*	*	*	*	*	*	*		*	*
Charlotte, First	*	*	*	*	*	*	*	*		*
Cleveland:										
Kistler's Union	*	*	*	*	*	*	*	*	*	*
Oak Grove	*	*	*	*	*	*	*	*	*	*
Lawndale	*	*	*	*	*	*	*	*	*	*
Mt. Pleasant	*	*	*	*	*	*	*	*	*	*
Mt. Moriah	*					*	*			
Concord	*	*	*	*	*	*	*	*	*	*
Creswell:										
Creswell	*	*								
Mt. Hermon	*									
Danville	*	*	*		*	*	*	*	*	*
Democrat										
Pleasant Gap	*		*	*	*	*	*			
Mountain Valley	*		*	*	*	*	*			
Denton:										
Denton	*	*	*	*	*	*	*		*	*
Canaan	*	*	*	*	*	*	*		*	*
Davidson										
Chapel Hill	*	*	*	*	*	*	*		*	*
Liberty	*	*	*	*	*	*	*		*	*
Pleasant Grove	*	*			*	*				*
Pine Hill	*	*	*			*				*
Alleghany	*									*
Lineberry	*	*				*				*
Draper	*	*	*	*	*	*				
Enfield-Whitakers										
Enfield	*	*	*	*	*	*	*	*	*	*
Whitakers	*	*	*	*	*	*	*	*	*	*

CHARGE OR CHURCH	Pastor's Salary	World Service	A. C. Expense	A. C. Debt	Church Extension	Superannuates	H. P. College	Herald Quota	Herald Subsidy	N. C. C. Rel. Ed.
Forsyth:										
Maple Springs	*	*	*	*	*	*	*		*	
Hickory Ridge	*	*	*		*	*	*			
Mt. Carmel	*					*	*			
Union Ridge	*					*	*			
Friendship-Love's Grove:										
Friendship							*	*		
Love's Grove	*		*			*	*			
Gibsonville	*		*	*	*	*	*		*	*
Graham	*		*	*		*	*	*	*	*
Granville:										
Union Chapel	*		*			*		*		
Rehoboth	*					*		*		
Mt. Carmel	*					*		*		
Calvary, Greensboro	*	*	*	*	*	*	*	*	*	*
West End, Greensboro	*	*				*		*	*	
St. Paul, Greensboro	*					*				
Grace, Greensboro	*							*		
Greensville										
Ebenezer	*		*	*	*	*				
Wesley's Chapel	*		*	*	*	*	*			
Mathews Chapel	*		*	*	*	*				
Philadelphia	*			*	*	*				
Hobbs Chapel	*			*		*				
Halifax:										
Bethesda	*	*	*	*	*	*	*			*
Eden	*	*	*	*	*	*	*			*
Union	*	*	*	*	*	*	*			
Holister						*				
Haw River:										
Friendship	*		*	*	*	*	*	*	*	*
Fair Grove	*									
Mizpah	*									
Henderson	*	*	*	*	*	*	*	*	*	*
High Point, First	*	*	*	*	*	*	*		*	*
High Point, Lebanon	*		*			*				
High Point, Rankin	*									
High Point, Welch	*	*	*	*	*	*	*	*		*
Kanhapolis	*		*	*	*	*	*	*	*	*
Lexington:										
First	*	*	*	*	*	*	*			*
Mt. Carmel	*	*	*							
Lexington, State St.	*			*		*	*			
Bethesda	*					*				

CHARGE OR CHURCH	Pastor's Salary	World Service	A. C. Expense	A. C. Debt	Church Extension	Superannuates	H. P. College	Herald Quota	Herald Subsidy	N. C. C. Rel. Ed.
Liberty	*	*	*	*	*	*	*	*	*	*
Lincolnton	*									
Fairfield	*									
Littleton:										
Littleton	*		*	*	*	*	*			
Hawkins Chapel	*					*				
Corinth						*				
Vaughn						*				
Weavers Chapel						*				
Mebane	*	*	*	*	*	*	*		*	*
Mecklenburg:										
Stallings	*		*	*						
New Hope	*		*	*	*	*				
Antioch	*		*	*	*	*				
Beulah	*		*	*	*					
Zoar	*									
Midland:										
Mill Grove	*						*			
Pine Bluff	*						*			
Midway	*	*	*	*	*	*	*	*	*	*
Mocksville:										
Elbaville	*		*	*	*	*			*	
Bethel			*	*			*			
Mt. Hermon:										
Bellemont	*	*	*	*	*	*	*		*	*
Cedar Cliff	*		*			*			*	*
Friendship	*	*	*	*	*	*	*		*	*
Mt. Hermon	*		*	*	*	*	*		*	*
Mt. Pleasant:										
Mt. Pleasant	*	*	*	*	*	*	*		*	*
Pleasant Union	*	*	*	*	*	*	*		*	*
Mt. Zion	*									
North Davidson:										
Spring Hill	*									*
Canaan	*	*	*			*				
West End				*		*			*	*
Mt. Pleasant										*
Orange:										
Efland	*	*	*	*	*	*	*		*	*
Union Grove	*								*	*
Hebron	*								*	
Chestnut Ridge	*		*	*	*	*				
Pensacola	*							*	*	
Pleasant Grove	*	*	*	*	*	*	*			*

CHARGE OR CHURCH	Pastor's Salary	World Service	A. C. Expense	A. C. Debt	Church Extension	Superannuates	H. P. College	Herald Quota	Herald Subsidy	N. C. C. Rel. Ed.
Pinnacle-Mt. Zion:										
Mt. Zion	*					*				
Pilot	*					*				
Pinnacle	*					*				
Shoals	*					*				
Porter	*	*								
Randolph:										
Gray's Chapel	*		*		*	*				
Bethel	*	*	*		*	*				
Bethany	*		*		*	*				
Shiloh	*	*				*				
Reidsville	*	*	*	*	*	*	*	*	*	*
Richland:										
Browers	*	*	*	*						
Charlotte	*	*	*	*						
Cedar Falls	*	*	*	*						
Giles Chapel	*	*	*	*						
New Union	*	*	*	*						
Randleman:										
Mt. Lebanon	*		*	*	*	*				
Worthville	*		*	*	*	*				
New Salem	*		*	*	*	*				
Level Cross	*		*	*	*	*				
Roberta	*	*	*	*		*			*	*
Rockingham:										
Rockingham	*	*	*			*	*			
Bethesda	*		*			*				
Pageland	*						*			
Saxapahaw:										
Saxapahaw	*	*	*	*	*	*	*		*	*
Concord	*									
Orange Chapel	*									
Salem	*		*	*	*					
Seagrove-Love Joy:										
Fairgrove	*					*				
Flint Hill						*				
Love Joy	*									
Macedonia	*					*				
Seagrove	*	*	*	*	*	*	*		*	*
Shelby-Caroleen	*					*				
Shiloh:										
Shiloh	*	*	*	*	*	*	*	*	*	*
Friendship	*	*	*	*	*	*	*		*	*
Greers Chapel	*		*	*	*	*			*	*

HONOR ROLL OF CHURCHES AND CHARGES

CHARGE OR CHURCH	Pastor's Salary	World Service	A. C. Expense	A. C. Debt	Church Extension	Superannuates	H. P. College	Herald Quota	Herald Subsidy	N. C. C. Rel. Ed.
Siler City:										
Siler City	*	*	*	*	*		*	*	*	*
Piney Grove	*	*	*	*	*	*	*	*	*	*
Hope	*						*		*	*
Spencer	*					*			*	
Spring Church:										
Spring Church	*					*			*	*
Lebanon	*					*			*	*
Pleasant Hill	*					*			*	*
Tabernacle-Julian	*	*	*	*	*	*	*	*	*	*
Thomasville, Com.	*		*	*	*	*	*		*	*
Thomasville, First	*	*	*	*	*	*	*	*	*	*
Vance:										
Spring Valley	*	*	*	*	*	*	*	*		
New Hope	*	*	*	*	*	*	*			
Flat Rock	*	*	*	*	*	*	*	*		
Gilburg	*	*	*	*	*	*	*			
West Forsyth:										
Stony Knoll	*		*	*	*	*	*			
Baltimore	*		*	*	*	*	*			
Harmony Grove	*									
Why Not:										
Piney Grove	*		*	*	*	*				
New Zion	*		*	*	*	*				
Flag Springs	*		*	*	*	*				
Pleasant Hill	*		*	*	*	*				
New Hope	*		*	*	*	*				
Winston, First	*	*	*	*	*	*	*	*	*	*
Yarborough:										
Yarborough Chapel								*		*
Harmony	*	*	*	*			*	*		*

STATISTICAL TABLES

TABLE I. CHURCH PROPERTY

HARGE	No. Organized Churches	No. Church Buildings	Church — Estimated Value	Church — Present Indebtedness	Church — Insured For	Other Church Property	No. of Parsonages	Parsonage — Estimated Value	Parsonage — Present Indebtedness	Parsonage — Insured For	Church Papers Taken
....	4	4	11,000	....	2,500	1,200	...	....	....	....	25
....	1	1	40,000	13 500	16,500	....	1	3,000	....	1,500	20
....	2	2	5,000	....	2,000	....	2	3,500	....	2,000	28
....	1	1	20,000	....	15,000	....	1	6,000	....	4,000	52
....	1	1	30,000	....	1,500	....	1	8,500	....	500	7
City..........	1	1	2,500	....	1,500	....	...	....	....	....	8
el.............	1	1	11,000	70	2,000	....	....	....	....	....	6
mit............	1	1	1,000	....	....	....	....	....	....	....	6
....	1	2	10,000	....	5,000	....	1	5,000	....	2,300	60
....	1	2	35,000	....	3,500	2,823	1	10,000	5,400	3,500	35
....	1	1	800	....	....	....	...	....	....	....	....
....	3	3	2,800	....	....	....	...	....	....	....	4
....	5	4	12,000	838	3,800	....	1	4,000	....	1,500	64
....	1	1	20,000	....	8,000	....	1	2,500	....	1,500	19
prings........	3	3	2,000	....	800	....	1	700	....	....	1
....	5	5	5,000	....	....	....	1	2,000	....	....	6
....	1	....	....	....	....	150	...	....	....	....	19
....	6	6	8,000	....	1,800	....	1	1,400	....	1,000	10
....	2	4	2,000	....	....	....	1	800	....	....	2
....	2	2	14,000	....	6,000	....	1	2,000	....	1,000	13
....	1	1	2,000	900	1,500	....	...	....	....	....	6
....	2	2	18,000	....	....	....	1	5,000	....	1.500	30
....	5	5	20,000	....	3,000	....	1	1,500	....	800	20
....	5	5	20,000	2,000	4,000	....	1	2,500	....	1,000	30
-Loves Grove.	2	2	9,000	....	3,000	....	1	3,500	....	....	9
....	5	5	50,000	....	15,000	....	1	5,000	....	2,500	20
lace..........	1	1	15,000	5,500	1,000	....	1	3,000	3,000	2,000	8
....	1	1	5,000	....	3,500	....	...	....	....	....	22
1..............	3	3	12,000	82	8,000	....	2	3,500	....	2,500	26
....	1	1	8,000	....	5,000	....	...	....	....	....	55
....	3	3	10,000	....	4,600	....	1	3,000	....	1,000	67
—Calvary.....	1	2	50,000	4,890	10,000	....	1	3,500	1,970	3,000	54
—Grace.......	1	1	150,000	53,649	45,500	....	2	12,000	4,600	10,000	32
St. Paul.....	1	1	4,000	....	....	....	...	....	....	....	8
West End..	1	1	23,500	10,400	12,000	....	...	....	....	....	35
....	5	5	10,000	....	....	....	1	1,500	....	1.000	42
....	4	4	15,000	....	8,500	....	1	1,500	....	1,000	8
....	6	6	13,000	....	5,500	500	1	2,000	....	....	22
....	4	4	23,000	....	8,000	1,500	1	4,500	175	2,000	50
....	1	1	50,000	....	12,500	....	1	6,000	....	1,500	38
t—First....	1	1	95,000	60,000	80,000	....	1	18,500	....	10,000	69
t—Lebanon....	1	1	15,000	....	5,000	....	...	....	....	....	....
Rankin Mem..	1	1	13,000	3,800	3,000	....	...	....	....	....	8
Welch Mem..	1	1	21,400	744	3,000	....	1	1,400	....	1,000	20
....	1	1	2,000	....	1,000	....	1	1,700	....	800	28
ə—S. Win.....	5	5	21,000	....	7,000	....	1	4,500	....	....	18
First........	2	2	8,000	....	3,500	....	...	....	....	....	26
State St........	3	3	30,000	13,000	1,400	....	1	8,000	....	4,000	26
....	1	1	7,000	1,200	1,500	....	1	5,000	....	1,500	14
-Fairfield........	2	2	10,000	2,000	3,000	....	...	....	....	....	17
....	5	5	5,000	....	....	100	1	1,500	....	1,000	16
....	1	1	5,000	....	3,000	....	1	2,500	....	1,500	12
rg............	5	5	5,300	....	....	....	1	1,000	....	....	....
....	2	2	1,500	....	....	....	1	1,500	....	1,200	10

TABLE I. CHURCH PROPERTY

HARGE	No. Organized Churches	No. Church Buildings	Church Estimated Value	Present Indebtedness	Insured For	Other Church Property	No. of Parsonages	Parsonage Estimated Value	Present Indebtedness	Insured For	Church Papers Taken
....	1	1	3,000	....	2,500	....	....	....	....	....	7
....	5	5	5,000	....	2,500	....	2	2,000	....	1,200	12
n...................	1	1	5,000	....	2,000	....	1	2,500	350	1,000	....
n...................	4	4	10,000	....	6,000	....	1	1,500	....	750	40
nt...................	3	3	9,500	....	5,350	....	1	2,000	....	1,000	36
....	3	3	2,100	....	700	....	....	....	....	....	4
idson...............	4	4	30,000	2,000	10,000	....	1	2,500	177	1,000	15
....	4	4	20,000	....	7,200	....	1	3,500	....	1,500	35
....	1	1	1,500	....	....	100	1	500	....	....	9
Mt. Zion.......	4	4	10,000	....	....	....	1	3,000	....	....	12
rove...............	1	1	10,000	....	2,500	....	1	5,000	....	2,500	8
....	1	1	4,000	....	....	....	....	....	....	....	9
....	4	4	10,000	....	4,000	....	1	2,500	....	1,500	12
....	4	4	10,000	....	....	....	1	700	....	....	16
....	1	1	10,000	....	5,000	....	1	5,500	....	4,200	12
....	5	5	6,000	....	3,000	....	1	1,500	....	750	1
....	1	1	3,500	....	1,500	....	1	2,000	....	1,000	15
....	4	4	5,000	....	....	....	....	....	....	....	....
....	4	4	6,000	85	4,000	....	1	1,800	....	1,200	17
ove Joy.........	5	5	27,000	....	....	....	1	1,500	400	1,000	10
e...................	1	1	5,000	....	....	....	....	....	....	....	....
oleen...............	2	2	6,000	....	....	....	1	1,200	364	1,200	13
....	3	3	20,000	....	9,500	....	1	3,500	500	2,000	44
....	3	3	10,000	....	....	....	....	....	....	....	21
ina Grove......	2	2	3,500	2,483	500	....	....	....	....	....	4
rch...............	3	2	4,000	200	2,000	....	1	2,000	....	1,500	12
....	2	2	8,000	....	4,200	....	1	1,500	....	600	40
e—Com.........	1	1	75,000	....	20,000	....	1	5,000	....	....	16
e—First.........	1	1	4,000	....	1,500	....	1	2,500	....	1,000	25
....	5	5	19,500	300	6,500	....	1	2,500	....	1,000	22
e...................	3	3	8,000	....	....	....	1	2,500	....	....	6
yth...............	6	6	8,500	....	....	....	1	1,800	....	....	12
....	1	1	15,000	....	....	....	1	4,000	....	1,800	25
....	5	5	11,000	....	1,000	....	....	....	....	....	13
First...............	1	1	50,000	....	10,000	....	1	3,500	....	1,200	30
....	2	2	5,000	....	1,500	....	....	....	....	....	15
Total...............	228	230	1,418,900	165,941	441,150	6,373	69	216,000	16,936	98,520	1,799

CHARGE

Number	CHARGE	No. Members													
1	Alamance	48	1	99	4	30	1	16	1	25	1	422	426	48	4
2	Albemarle	40	2	175	1	15	1			75	2	225	160	52	1
3	Anderson			15	1			15	1			250	250	25	2
4	Asheboro			12	1	22	1	18	1	30	2	443	475	52	6
5	Asheville			38	1							150	150	11	1
6	Bessemer City			17	1					10	1	127	120	9	1
7	Bess Chapel			260	1	12	1	20	1	44	1	120	100	9	1
8	Brown Summit			190	1	36	1	40	1	25	1	120	124	9	1
9	Burlington											136	509	38	1
10	Charlotte	40	1	10	1	12	1			25	1	592	459	35	3
11	Chase City			38	3							611	40	6	4
12	Chatham	12	1	110	1	23	1	30	1	12	1	40	120	15	3
13	Cleveland			14	1					25	1	120	450	41	5
14	Concord			25	1							507	433	25	1
15	Connelly Springs			12	1					10	1	428	200	16	6
16	Creswell	35	1	50	2	15	1	30	1	20	1	239	140	22	2
17	Danville	15	1							40	1	150	130	9	2
18	Davidson			41	1							135	368	48	1
19	Democrat	85	3	96	1					50	3	370	120	14	5
20	Denton									18	1	93	260	25	1
21	Draper	85	4	60	1	10	1			20	1	280	69	6	2
22	Enfield			14	1					35	1	90	85	11	1
23	Fallston	85	2	50	1	15	1					85	397	44	5
24	Flat Rock			180	3			25	1	39	1	405	397	32	4
25	Friendship-Loves Grove	40	2	100	1	15	1			13	1	353	286	18	2
26	Forsyth			70	1			15	1			283	500	40	5
27	Fountain Place			15	1							505		10	1
28	Gibsonville	15	1									110	204	18	1
29	Glen Raven											212	430	30	3
30	Graham											450	150	22	1
31	Granville											160	360	28	3
32	Greensboro—Calvary											360	294	30	1
33	Greensboro—Grace											290	192	19	1
34	Greensboro—St. Paul											180	150	9	1

106

																																							Total
13	22	28	36	30	18	44	10			38		20		20	28		11	50	20				12			34				1009
1	1	1	3	2	1	2	1			3		1	1		1	1	1			1			2							48
	151		10	70	60		13	110		50	22		40	66	60		35	20		42	55	60	8		35	150	50	56	64	12	45	20	20	90	12				3962
	1		1	3	2		1	4		3	1		1	1	3		2	1		3	2	1	1	1	2	1	1	3	1	2	1	1	1	1					96
30						15					15	25					43			7										386
1						1					1	1					1					1								20
	20				13	15									25		48		10											317
	1				1	1									1		2		1											16
66		40		24	82		20	79		60		37	35	40			25		65	25	50		37	65	23		15		28	62	30		20	30					1783
2		2		1	2		1	3		3		1	1	1			1		2	1	2		1	1	1		1		1	1	1		1	1					68
262	95	215	300	130	150	422	178	583	423	207	500	374	71	495	224	70	470	420	170	290	175	551	380	30	140	590	200	84	183	250	150	345	360	140	655	70	160	98	24551
240	150	215	300		149	446	146	514	425	200	428	399	70	490	164	65	474	490	160	295	144	535	375	30	130	600	200	65	220	244	200	296	332	180	650	68	175	93	23774
19	14	15	30	11	8	57	10	43	24	21	32	36	10	16	16	11	33	32	12	13	26	56	42	4	16	65	23	12	26	28	19	15	37	20	34	11	19	17	2171
2	2	1	4	2	1	5	1	4	3	3	4	4	1	4	1	1	4	4	1	1	3	4	5	1	2	3	3	2	3	2	1	1	5	3	6	1	1	2	211
3		1		2		1				2		7		1		6		1		1		1		2		1		1		92
10	15	5	14	3	8	4	12	15	9	3	8	21	8	4	9	16	4	9	18	6	4	4	9	10	2	4	13	31	42	2	27	5	6	6	5				1051
208	465	266	308	198	70	456	179	978	618	171	356	752	60	565	157	55	502	774	126	450	287	211	586	352	174	650	212	68	335	393	169	252	537	194	675	77	383	262	98	30831
6	71	20	4	8	6	2	8	74	15	16	19	8	18	6	26	4	6	12	27	20	3	15	10	7	16	8	1	3	2	1	3	11	4	1095
37	15	12	22	5	7	12	6	19	19	9	17	5	23	14	5	12	19	7	19	22	5	17	9	17	18	12	10	14	5	17	41	47	3	27	3	7	10		1824
63	17	5	62	10	4	14	4	20	22	23	15	40	10	21	40	10	17	41	5	14	31	26	25	72	29	12	5	10	33	13	60	57	3	30		20	6	40	2769
177	521	274	290	201	69	446	181	1033	614	164	365	754	55	550	161	50	496	781	123	431	271	219	596	363	160	647	202	66	328	404	160	212	493	193	655	75	379	263	93	29899
		1		1		1	2		1					1	1	3	1	1				1				1		1	1	1				57

Number	CHARGE	Apportioned for "World Service"	Paid by Mem Direct	Raised by Wo Auxiliary	Raised for Conference	For Annual Conf. Deb	For Church Extensio	For Superannuates	Total Paid for Other Conference Interests
1	Alamance	550	10	119	198	22	35	21	216
2	Albemarle	430	4		10	3	5	10	52
3	Anderson	30	6	100	10	35	35	15	81
4	Asheboro	665		280	351	35	35	54	700
5	Asheville	390		35	43	6	8		81
6	Bessemer City	25		5	5			5	12
7	Bess Chapel	500		40	50				47
8	Brown Summit	25							15
9	Burlington	600		440	600	66	66	60	951
10	Charlotte	200	70	130	200	25	25	46	389
11	Chase City	50				3	2	2	
12	Chatham	110	2	24	6			45	6
13	Cleveland	850	17	139	50	55	55		34
14	Concord	540	150		309			45	348
15	Connelly Springs	200							
16	Creswell	525		5	5	7	6	3	50
17	Danville	75	5		20	2	12	27	113
18	Davidson	645		17	21	16	1	22	29
19	Democrat	110				6	16	4	
20	Denton	455	5		46	14	6	21	198
21	Draper	150		45	5	14	14	15	
22	Enfield	250		65	87	8	12	25	238
23	Fallston	125			65	15		15	185
24	Flat Rock	69		1	6	18	5	21	75
25	Friendship-Loves Grove	320	5		6		18	8	120
26	Forsyth	500		107	112	15	15	48	445
27	Fountain Place			34	52	10		24	148
28	Gibsonville	100	100	89	97	17	2	24	296
29	Glen Raven	450						41	123
30	Graham	150		62	126	15		45	184
31	Granville	200		150	178	10	20	45	389
32	Greensboro—Calvary	620		115	265	20	20	20	334
33	Greensboro—Grace	640		163	213	5	5	20	250
34	Greensboro—St. Paul	490		19	19	7	15	36	72

Number	Charge															Grand Total
1	Alamance	1,100	1,074	1,200	366			60				144	146		1,805	2,415
2	Albemarle	900	1,100	1,200	100	1,600	941	200				339	105	536	4,931	5,018
3	Anderson	300	900	900	1,800	1,800								175	3,175	3,266
4	Asheboro	1,800	1,800	2,000			42	59		400	550	749	1,116	773	5,504	6,859
5	Asheville	1,200	1,084	1,200	13	200				14			196	86	1,443	1,567
6	Bessemer City	400	300	350		50		100			215	50	125	120	.708	850
7	Bess Chapel	300	300	350		1,122		100				50	97	244	2,093	2,210
8	Brown Summit	200	200	200				15				66	35		316	349
9	Burlington	2,250	2,250	2,250				1,471	342	288		1,318	1,098	350	7,127	9,145
10	Charlotte		2,600	2,600	1,631	500		3,010		145	180	1,852	1,148	316	11,562	12,397
11	Case City		100	100												
12	Chatham	175	163	175	121			5				17		72	278	307
13	Cleveland	1,400	1,405	1,400	25	75				116					1,681	1,765
14	Concord	1,400	1,400	1,400				236		114		228	480	114	2,458	3,480
15	C...ely Springs	350	252	350						17		16	179	73	509	515
16	Creswell	632	609	632				110		10	31	25	154	15	938	,008
17	Danville	900	900	960	537			5				505			2,007	2,218
18	Davidson	1,000	1,000	1,000			8	35		15	2	125	86	15	1,286	1,434
19	Democrat	250	250	150											250	266
20	Denton	950	950	950				91		20		176	151	39	1,432	1,814
21	Draper	700	700	700		100	45					25	44		914	963
22	Enfield	938	938	825				100		40		50	62	182	1,372	1,697
23	Fallston	1,250	1,205	1,250	3,475		99	145		45		105	210	345	5,495	5,818
24	Flat Rock	0D	1,074	0D		300		47				54	109	187	1,915	2,052
25	Friendship-Loves Grove	850	850	850				60				88	125		1,235	1,477
26	Forsyth	,600	1,650	1,600				300	312	150		255	217	515	3,135	3,873
27	Fountain Place	600	600	500	892							80	40	40	2,149	2,354
28	Gibsonville	800	1,400	1,400	500	20		150				409	659	179	3,397	3,924
29	Glen Raven	1,200	1,235	1,200	200	8				220		300	500	400	2,888	3,225
30	Graham	1,350	1,350	1,350				62				636	162	78	2,309	2,791
31	Granville	1,500	1,500	,50D				75				260	130	55	2,020	2,722
32	...—Calvary	1,500	1,500	1,50D	607	321					243	300	408	900	4,423	5,227
33	Greensboro—Grace	1,650	1,650	1,650	300	350	1,600	80		50	257	853	394	129	5,663	6,226
34	Greensboro—St. Paul	1,200	1,200	1,200							129	308	308	85	1,593	1,738

No.	Name	Value
38	Halifax	1,917
39	Haw River	3,378
40	Henderson	2,983
41	High Point—First	14,526
42	High Point—Lebanon	2,595
43	High Pt.—Rankin Dem	2,520
44	High Pt.—Welch Mem	4,364
45	Kannapolis	2,806
46	Kernersville—S. Win	1,765
47	Lexington—First	2,963
48	Lexington—State St	2,982
49	Liberty	2,673
50	Lincolnton-Fairfield	3,254
51	Littleton	809
52	Mebane	2,114
53	Mecklenburg	1,435
54	Midland	1,375
55	Midway	719
56	Mocksville	692
57	Moriah	1,290
58	Mt. Hermon	4,270
59	Mt. ... Mt	3,712
60	Mt. Zion	391
61	North Davidson	959
62	Orange	2,854
63	Pensacola	230
64	Pinnacle—Mt. Zion	680
65	Pleasant Grove	3,040
66	Porter	186
67	Randleman	2,200
68	Randolph	1,782
69	Reidsville	2,853
70	Richland	1,928
71	Roberta	1,674
72	Rockingham	1,831
73	Saxapahaw	2,837
74	Seagrove-Love Joy	2,107
75	Shady-Grove	128
77	Shiloh	4,288
78	Siler City	890
79	Spencer-China	477
80	Spring Church	3,947
81	Tabernacle	2,420
82	Thomasville—Com	3,424
83	Thomasville—First	3,002
84	Vance	2,404
85	Weaverville	1,390
86	West th	1,685
87	Whitakers	1,542
88	Why Not	1,643
89	Winston—First	3,410
90	Yarborough	806

APPORTIONMENTS

CHARGE	W. Service	A. C. Exp.	A. C. D.	Ch. Ext.	Super.	College
Alamance ....$	550	$110	$48	$48	$32	$ 75
Albemarle	430	35	14	14	27	60
Anderson	300	33	15	15	24	38
Asheboro	665	80	35	35	54	100
Asheville	390	25	13	13	28	35
Bess Chapel....................	500	20	10	10	13	60
Bessemer City.................	25	8	4	5	10	25
Brown Summit.................	25	8	4	4	6	25
Burlington, First............	825	150	66	66	60	125
Burlington, Ft. Place.....	275	20	10	10	18	35
Caroleen-Shelby	100	10	5	5	12 ·	30
Charlotte	430	50	25	25	46	100
Chase City.......................	50	10	· 5	5	8	25
Chatham	110	16	8	8	10	25
Cleveland	850	75	34	34	42	75
Concord	540	110	55	55	42	100
Connelly Springs.............	200	8	4	4	9	25
Creswell	525	25	13	13	15	35
Danville	75	12	6	6	27	75
Davidson	645	55	25	25	28	60
Democrat	110	4	2	2	5	10
Denton	455	35	16	16	21	50
Draper	150	12	6	6	15	25
Enfield	250	28	14	14	25	50
Fallston	125	55	25	25	36	75
Flat Rock......................	690	85	45	45	33	75
Friendship-Love Grove...	300	30	15	15	14	50
Forsyth	500	75	35	35	48	75
Gibsonville	320	30	15	15	24	50
Glen Raven	450	30	15	15	36	75
Graham	450	37	17	17	41	75
Granville	600	110	55	55	45	85
Greensboro, Calvary.......	620	40	20	20	45	80
Greensboro, Grace...........	640	70	35	35	50	100
Greensboro, St. Paul......	400	30	15	15	36	50
Greensboro, W. End........	400	30	15	15	30	75
Greensville	500	30	15	15	30	60
Guilford	500	30	15	15	26	60
Halifax	600	60	30	30	36	75
Haw River......................	750	45	25	25	46	75
Henderson	700	50	25	25	41	100
High Point, First............	1100	150	67	67	72	300
High Point, Lebanon......	535	55	25	25	38	100
High Pt., Rankin Ml......	75	25	13	13	20	50
High Pt., Welch Ml........	300	44	22	22	36	75
Kannapolis	· 225	· 20	10	· 10	21	25
Kernersville-S. Win........	300	33	15	15	27	60
Lexington, First............	350	40	20	20	45	60
Lexington, Bethesda........	450	33	15	15	32	50
Liberty·	350	30	15	15	18	25
Lincolnton	300	30 ·	15	15	25 ·.	50
Littleton	350	40	20	20	19 ˉ	60
Mebane	325	33	15	15	30	60
Mecklenburg	325	33	15	15	17	60
Midland	540	33	15	15	22	60

CHARGE	W. Service	A. C. Exp.	A. C. D.	Ch. Ext.	Super.	College
Midway	150	10	5	5	6	25
Mocksville	300	40	20	20	25	30
Mill Grove	100	8	4	4	5	15
Moriah	225	25	12	12	16	40
Mt. Ebal	25	4	2	2	5	10
Mt. Hermon	900	90	45	45	38	100
Mt. Pleasant	750	82	41	41	36	75
Mt. Zion	50	15	8	8	10	25
North Davidson	520	50	25	25	25	80
Orange	750	90	45	45	45	80
Pensacola	75	10	5	5	4	10
Pine Bluff	100	6	3	3	....	12
Pinnacle-Mt. Zion	600	50	35	25	30	65
Pleasant Grove	400	50	25	25	15	65
Porter	75	4	2	2	3	10
Randleman	400	50	25	25	30	65
Randolph	500	70	35	35	35	100
Reidsville	450	22	11	11	45	50
Richland	500	33	15	15	24	65
Roberta	320	33	15	15	27	50
Rockingham	180	20	10	10	19	35
Saxapahaw	350	55	25	25	34	60
Seagrove-Love Joy	450	45	23	23	22	50
Shiloh	750	55	27	27	45	60
Siler City	350	50	25	25	24	60
Spencer-China Grove	50	10	5	5	2	15
Spring Church	500	50	25	25	32	65
Tabernacle	550	66	33	33	33	75
Thomasville, Com.	400	66	33	33	54	100
Thomasville, First	450	44	22	22	36	60
Vance	450	55	27	27	37	75
Weaverville	250	18	9	9	27	30
West Forsyth	350	55	27	27	25	50
Whitakers	190	18	9	9	15	50
Why Not	450	38	19	19	17	50
Winston, First	450	50	25	25	38	70
Yarborough	160	15	8	8	13	30

Note:—The apportionment for Superannuates is based on 3 per cent of the salary received for the year 1934-35. (See report of President and Committee on President's Message.)

The second quarterly conference of each pastoral charge shall nominate double the number of laymen to which the charge-circuit or station—is entitled as delegates to the Annual Conference. The pastor shall announce from each pulpit the names of nominees, and appoint a day, which shall be that on which his appointment shall fall at each church if practicable, for taking the vote by ballot for the number to which the charge may be entitled; the ballots cast by members over eighteen years of age to be received by class leaders and stewards, under the supervision of the pastor and by them to be counted, and the count forwarded to the third quarterly conference, to be compared by that body. The nominee receiving the plurality of vote shall be declared duly elected, and the pastor immediately shall certify to the Secretary of the Annual Conference the delegate elected, and such certified list shall constitute the lay roll of this Conference.

The alternate delegate shall be elected by the fourth quarterly Conference.

Only qualified members—those who are twenty-one years of age or over—shall be allowed to vote to purchase, build, repair, lease, sell, rent, mortgage, or otherwise procure or dispose of church property.

WHERE TO SEND YOUR MONEY

For Herald Subscriptions and Subsidy: Make remittances payable to METHODIST PROTESTANT HERALD, not to individuals. Send to Methodist Protestant Herald, Box 1950, Greensboro, N. C.

For World Service and Conference Interests: Offerings for Special Days and for the Annual Conference Budget and the College Apportionment: Make checks payable to J. H. Allen, Treasurer, and mail to him at Reidsville, N. C. (Do not send any money direct to the General Conference Treasurer.)

For North Carolina Branch of Woman's Work: For North Carolina Work, and for World Service. Make checks payable to Mrs. W. A. Hornaday, and send to her address—Box 402, Greensboro, N. C.

If you will observe these simple suggestions it will help keep our accounts straight, and enable you to get proper credit.

ERENCE

shall

The

and

shall

for

by

aders

them to

the

in-

ce

ay

quarterly

age or

ease,

church

pay-

Seed to

for

he College

ney I felt

Car-

Mrs.

nsboro,

keep our

CPSIA information can be obtained
at www.ICGtesting.com
Printed in the USA
BVHW040001291118
534010BV00050B/560/P